GUIDE TO THE

Roger Caldwell

Emerald Guides

Emerald Guides

© Straightforward Co Ltd 2020

British Cataloguing in Publication data. A catalogue record is available for this book from the British Library.

ISBN

978-1-913342-47-0

Printed in the United Kingdom by 4edge Ltd www.4edge.co.uk

Cover Design by Straightforward Graphics

Contents

List of cases

Chapter 2-Negligence and causation

Chapter 3- Contributory Negligence

Chapter 4- Employers Liability

Chapter 7- Liability for dangerous/Defective Goods

Chapter 8- Nuisance

Chapter 9- Defamation

Chapter 10- Strict Liability

Chapter 11-Liability for animals

****

Introduction

A Guide to the Law of Tort is updated to **2020**. The law of tort is one of the main, or core, subjects taught on law courses and it involves, as does criminal law, a two-stage process: the imposition of liability and the availability or otherwise of a defence.

Tort covers a very wide range of issues that are relevant to aspects of everyday life, such as employment and the working environment generally, disputes between neighbours, injuries sustained whilst on another's premises and libel and slander.

Medical negligence whilst always a growing area, will particularly be so now with the advent of the Coronavirus and the fear of what might happen later with a whole host of claimants coming forward. A discussion of medical negligence and the coronavirus is in chapter 1. There is also likely to be a spate of claims of negligence in relation to care homes and the general duty of care.

The Defamation Act 2013 is discussed which attempts to bring some sort of balance into the law affecting this area.

This book will be particularly useful to students of law, as it is concise and covers topics central to law examinations. It will also be useful to all those who wish to gain a general overview of the law and tort, of negligence generally.

Tort is a vast area and this brief introduction is aimed at those who wish to obtain a general insight before embarking on the main textbooks covering the area. This book introduces the reader to the concept of negligence, causation and remoteness of damage, contributory negligence, liability of employers, vicarious liability, occupiers liability, dangerous products, nuisance, defamation, strict liability and liability for animals. Overall, the reader will get a comprehensive overview of the law of tort and a firm grasp of the main principles.

****

Ch.1

Negligence and Duty of Care –Breach of Duty

In everyday parlance, negligence means a failure to pay attention to what ought to be done or to take the required level of care. Whereas its everyday usage implies a state of mind, the tort of negligence is concerned with the link between the defendant's behaviour and the risk that should have been foreseen.

Key definition of negligence
Negligence as a tort is a breach of legal duty to take care which results in damage to the claimant.

Negligence, as a tort, is generally defined as a breach of a duty of care. This duty of care is owed by one person to another. When damage is caused to a person, who then becomes a claimant, the type of damage has to be specified and also defined as actionable.

The loss or damage can arise in a number of ways, arising through misfeasance or nonfeasance and can consist of personal injury, damage to property or can be pure economic loss. It can also consist of psychiatric damage.

The duty of care-establishment of a duty
Certain relationships between people, recognised by the law and developed by the law, give rise to a legal duty of care. The following are examples:
- Employer-employee

17

- Manufacturer to consumer
- Doctor-patient
- Solicitor-client

Essentially, carelessness by one party which affects another gives rise, or can give rise, to legal action by the injured party. It is up to the claimant to prove that damage has been caused and that the case falls into a specific situation that gives rise to a duty of care.

The neighbour principle
Donoghue v Stevenson 1932
Outside of the categories of established duty, a duty of care will be determined on the basis of individual circumstances.

One of the most prominent cases relating to Tort and negligence is that of *Donoghue v Stevenson* (HL 1932) In this case, Mrs Donoghue and friend visited a café and Mrs Donoghue's friend bought her a bottle of ginger beer. The bottle was made of opaque glass. When filling Mrs Donoghue's glass the remains of a decomposed a snail floated out of the bottle. Mrs Donoghue developed gastroenteritis as a result.

Mrs Donoghue brought an action against the manufacturer's of the ginger beer. Lord Atkin formulated a general principle in this case, the **neighbour principle**, for determining whether a duty of care should exist. He stated:

"You must take reasonable care to avoid acts or omissions which you can reasonably foresee would be likely to injure your neighbour. Who then, in law, is my neighbour? The answer seems to be persons who are so closely and directly affected by my act that I ought reasonably to have them in contemplation as being so affected when I am directing my mind to the acts or omissions which are called in question".

The manufacturers were found liable as they owed her a duty of care that the bottle did not contain foreign bodies which would damage her health.

This principle was a landmark and established negligence as an independent tort

Out of this judgement, which was further developed in the case of *Caparo Industries plc v Dickman* (1990), also comes the concept of foresight, i.e. was the damage itself reasonably foreseeable. There must be a legal relationship of 'sufficient proximity' between the parties. There is also a requirement that it is 'just and reasonable' to impose a duty on the defendant.

Caparo Industries purchased shares in Fidelity Plc with faith they would be successful as the accounts that the company stated showed the company had made a pre-tax profit of £1.3 million. However these accounts were not correct and in reality Fidelity had made a loss of £400,000. Caparo claimed Fidelity was negligent, however no duty of care was owed due to the insufficient proximity between Caparo and Fidelity. *Caparo v Dickman* is a key authority to cite when making submissions about proximity (which tends to be an argument raised by defendants in many negligence proceedings).

Even where the courts are prepared to find that the circumstances are such as to be capable of giving rise to a duty of care, it is still likely that the claimant in a case could fail if he or she was an 'unforeseeable victim' of the defendants negligence.

Two notable cases involving an alleged duty of care are:

David Topp v London County Bus (South West) Limited (1993)

A driver of a mini bus did not turn up to his shift. The mini bus was then stolen and the thieves proceeded to assault a woman by knocking her off her bicycle (she subsequently died from her injuries). The husband of the woman claimed that the bus company owed a duty of care, however it was found they did not owe a duty of care towards a third party.

Home Office v Dorset Yacht Co Ltd (1970)

Borstal officers were required to supervise young offenders who were working on Brown Sea Island, however the officers left the boys unsupervised. Several of the young offenders then stole a boat and crashed it into the yacht of the Claimant. It was found the Home Office owed a duty of care as they were in a position of control over the 3rd party who caused the damage which was considered foreseeable by the court.

Another major case was *Bourhill v Young* (1943).

The Claimant was pregnant and disembarked a tram, the defendant then got into a car accident on his motorbike 50 feet away and was killed on impact. The Claimant, a short time later proceeded to walk past where the incident had taken place and saw a large amount of blood where the incident had taken place, causing her to go into shock and her baby was still born. She brought a negligence claim against the Defendant's estate however no duty of care was owed by the Defendant to the Claimant.

Essentially, the legal proximity of claimant to defendant must be clearly established. In *Davis v Radcliffe* (1990), for example, Lord Goff stated that proximity referred to such a relation between the parties as rendered it just and reasonable that a duty should be imposed. Lack of proximity can, in some cases, be attributed to the failure of just and reasonable requirement in a case. A variety of factors are considered, such as the status of the parties and their relationship with one another, nature of injury or harm suffered and the particular way that the harm arises. One seminal case which further defined the boundaries of tort and negligence was that of *Hedley Byrne and Co v Heller and Partners Ltd* (1964). Lord Pearce observed:

"How wide the sphere of duty of care in negligence is to be laid depends primarily on the courts assessment of the demands of society for protection from the carelessness of others"

The case of Hedley Byrne concerned Economic loss through negligent information (see below).

Pure economic loss

Although financial loss incurred as a result of a negligent action against a person and property is normally recoverable, problems can arise with so called 'pure' economic loss, which is financial loss which has not been accompanied by any other damage. Cases of financial loss may arise as a result of either negligent information or advice, or of negligent conduct. In general, courts will assess these cases on a case-by-case basis, rather than rely purely on precedent.

Before the Hedley Byrne case, liability for negligent statements, or misstatements, which resulted in financial or other loss, existed in contract, in the tort of deceit or for breach of a fiduciary duty. In Hedley Byrne and Co v Heller and Partners Ltd the plaintiffs wanted to know if they could safely advance credit to their client, (A). The plaintiff's bankers sought references from the defendants (B) bankers, who gave favourable reports 'without responsibility'. The plaintiffs relied on the information and then suffered financial loss when A went into liquidation. In this case, it was held that no duty arose because of the disclaimer. However, importantly, in appropriate circumstances, a duty could arise.

It was accepted that reasonable foresight of the harm was not enough in itself, but that a 'special relationship' must exist where, to the defendants knowledge the plaintiff relied upon the defendants skill and judgement or his ability to make careful enquiry, and it was reasonable in the circumstances for the plaintiff to do so. The essence of Hedley and Byrne can therefore be equated with the concept of 'reasonable reliance'.

As discussed previously, another case highlighting the above is that of *Caparo Industries v Dickman 1990* where Lord Bridge said that in order for a duty to arise, it was necessary to show that the defendant knew that his statement would be communicated to the plaintiff, either as an individual or as a member of an identifiable class, specifically in connection with a transaction or transactions of a particular kind, and that the plaintiff would be very likely to rely on it in deciding whether or not to enter into a transaction.

Provided that the defendant is aware of the existence of the claimant either as an individual or as a member of an ascertainable class, there is no need that the defendant knows the identity of the claimant. A vital ingredient of the duty is the defendant's knowledge (actual or constructive) of the purpose for which the information is required. In Caparo Industries it was held that, in preparing the audit of the accounts of a public company, the defendants owed no duty either to the plaintiffs either as potential investors or as existing shareholders. The purpose of the audit was to report to the shareholders to enable them to exercise their rights in the management of the company, not to provide information which might assist them in making investment decisions.

In contrast to the position of auditors, surveyors appointed to value a house for mortgage purposes may owe a duty to the purchaser even though the primary purpose of the valuation is to enable the lender to decide whether to advance a loan. This was illustrated in *Harris v Wyre Forest District Council* (1989). This has been justified on the basis that valuers are paid for their services at the mortgagor's expense and understand that a lot of purchasers rely on these reports.

Contributory negligence (disclaimers)

On the assumption that an appropriately worded disclaimer is brought to the claimant's notice, either before or at the time the statement is made, it can be argued that no duty arises because the claimant's reliance would not be reasonable.

However, according to the House of Lords in the case *Smith v Eric S Bush* (1989), the effect of ss.11 (3) and 13 (1) of the Unfair Contract Terms Act 1977 is to subject all exclusion notices which would at common law provide a reasonable defence to an action for negligence, to a test of reasonableness, as provided for in s2 (2) of the act (this only relates to business liability).

Contributory negligence, which is discussed further in the book, is in principle a defence and is available equally to a claim under the Misrepresentation Act 1967.

Third party reliance

There are certain situations in which a duty of care will be imposed on a person (A), who makes a statement to B, as a result that B acts upon it to another's detriment. It is well established, generally, that a solicitor owes no duty of care to third parties. However, this is not always the case. For example, in *White v Jones* (1995), a majority of the House of Lords held the defendant solicitors liable for failing to carry out their clients instructions regarding his will, with the result that the plaintiffs (the intended beneficiaries) lost their legacy.

The duty under White v Jones is not confined to cases relating to wills. In *Gorham v British Telecommunications plc* (CA 2000) an insurance company was held to owe a duty of care to the customer's dependant wife and family where he had intended to create a benefit for them on his death. It was also held in *Spring v Guardian Assurance plc* (HL 1994) that an employer supplying a reference about an employee to a prospective employer owes a duty to the employee to avoid making untrue statements negligently or expressing unfounded opinions, even if held honestly and believed to be true. In this case, it was the opinion of the majority of the Lords that economic loss in the form of failure to obtain employment was clearly foreseeable if a careless reference was given and there was clear proximity of relationship as between employer and employee, so that it was fair, just and reasonable that the law should impose a duty on the employer.

Negligent acts

Although there was originally no liability for pure economic loss caused by acts of negligence, the Hedley Byrne case made major inroads into this area and, although this case was originally confined to misstatements, a trend has developed towards the formulation of a wider principle, applying to both statements and acts.

Damage to third party property

In some cases, damages to property belonging to a third party may prevent the claimant from carrying on their business. In other cases, their contract with the third party may be adversely affected. In neither case can the claimant recover any damages because of a long established rule that no claim will lie in respect of foreseeable economic loss, unaccompanied by physical damage to the property in which the claimant has an interest, either proprietary or possessory.

Defective property

If a claimant has acquired property and discovers it is defective, and money has to be spent on repairing or replacing it, such economic loss can be recovered against a party who has a relevant contractual obligation with the defendant. The claimant cannot bring a claim within the ordinary principles of tort, i.e. those contained within Donoghue v Stevenson, because the claim is concerned with defective goods which can cause personal injury or damage to property rather than the defective product in question.

However, although this was traditionally the case, this fundamental principle was brought into question in the case of *Anns v Merton London Borough Council* (HL 1978). While building a block of flats the foundations were made 2ft 6in deep instead of the required 3ft deep. This significant error caused the flats to have structural issues. Tenants of the block of flats claimed the Council was responsible for inspecting the foundations during construction. The House of Lords (the predecessor to the Supreme Court) held that the Council did owe a duty of care to ensure the foundations were at the correct depth.

Another case which developed this principle was *Junior Books Ltd v Veitchi Co Ltd* (HL 1983). The defendants were held liable for the cost of replacing a defective good supplied by them, even though there was no danger to health and safety. This decision went a considerable way to recognising a general right of recovery for pure economic loss. However, cases following this one have made it very clear that no new principle has been established and each case is viewed on its own merit.

Following a number of cases, the whole issue was considered by the Court of Appeal in *Murphy v Brentwood District Council* (HL 1990). The Lords unanimously overruled the findings in Anns so far as it imposed a duty on local authorities, on the ground that where a defect in a building was discovered before any personal injury or damage to property other than the defective house itself had been done, the expense incurred by the building owner in rectifying the defect (including associated costs such as vacating the premises) was pure economic loss and therefore irrecoverable in tort.

There are problems with the decision in Murphy, however. It would seem clear enough that the builder may be liable in accordance with Donoghue v Stevenson principles where a latent defect causes personal injury or damage to another property. In addition, it was thought, by one of the Lords reviewing the case, Lord Bridge, that where a building remained a potential source of injury to persons or property on neighbouring land or on the highway, the owner ought in principle be able to recover in tort from the negligent builder any costs incurred in order to protect himself from potential liabilities to third parties.

Most significantly, the Lords attached weight to the fact that it is the claimant's knowledge of the defect which makes the defect one of quality only, and therefore the loss purely economic. However, such knowledge has not necessarily barred the right of recovery.

One such case which highlighted this was *Rimmer v Liverpool City Council* (CA 1984). In this case, the designers and builders of a council flat, the local authority, was liable to a tenant injured by a pane of dangerously thin glass. The tenant knew of the danger and had complained, to no avail. It was considered that it was not practical for the tenant to either leave the flat or to change the pane of glass himself, although damages were reduced for contributory negligence.

Psychiatric illness

In *Alcock v Chief Constable of South Yorkshire* (HL 1991) Lord Ackner stated that shock "involves the sudden appreciation by sight or sound of a horrifying event, which violently agitates the mind". Shock must manifest itself in some recognisable psychiatric or physical illness. Mere grief or emotional upset is not actionable, although mental distress suffered as a result of negligently inflicted injuries may be taken into account in the assessment of damages for pain and suffering.

Shock victims fall into two (very) broad groups, those who are unwilling participants in the events causing shock (known as primary victims) and those who are merely passive and unwilling victims (secondary victims). In relation to the first group, Lord Ackner said that if the defendants negligent conduct foreseeably puts the plaintiff in that position it follows that there will be a sufficiently proximate relationship between them, though if personal injury of some kind to the plaintiff is reasonably foreseeable as the result of an accident the defendant is liable for psychiatric injury (even though no physical injury occurs) and the plaintiff need not prove that injury by shock was foreseeable because the defendant must take his victim as he finds him.

Subsequent cases have established three types of primary victim, namely those who are put in reasonable fear for their own safety, rescuers and those who reasonably believe that they are about to be, or have been, the involuntary cause of another's death or injury. Such persons will recover if shock to them was reasonably foreseeable or if personal injury of some kind was foreseeable. Where shock victims fall within the second category of groups a more complex analysis is required. It was held in Alcock that in order to recover damages, the plaintiff had to prove the following:

a) that his relationship to the primary victim was sufficiently close that it was reasonably foreseeable that he might suffer shock if he apprehended that the victim had been, or might be, injured;

b) that he was temporally and spatially close to the scene of the accident or its immediate aftermath;

c) that he suffered shock through sight or hearing of the accident or its immediate aftermath.

One matter not covered in Alcock was whether a plaintiff could recover for shock caused as a result of witnessing the destruction of property. In *Attia v British Gas plc* (CA 1988) it was held that there was no principle of law that shock in such circumstances could never be regarded as foreseeable. However, since the defendants in that case admitted to owing a duty in respect of the damage to the plaintiff's home, the shock issue was treated as one of remoteness rather than duty.

Omissions

In tort, as a general rule, the defendant does not owe a duty to take positive action to prevent harm to others. For example, the failure of a public authority to exercise a statutory power, or a statutory duty, will not normally give rise to a common law duty (see *Stovin v Wise* HL 1996). The mere existence of statutory powers and duties did not create a parallel common law duty. This was highlighted in the case of *Gorringe v Calderdale* (2004) where the highway authorities failure to paint a marking or to erect a road sign warning of a dangerous stretch of road did not give rise to a duty of care to the claimant.

Exceptions to the rule

The police

In performing the function of investigating and preventing crime, the police hold no duty of care to an individual member of the public. However, under the Human Rights Act 1998 (incorporating the European Convention on Human Rights into UK law) courts are required to balance whether the granting of immunity to a defendant is proportionate to the interference with the claimants human rights. Therefore, the police do not have total immunity.

In the case *Swinney v Chief Constable of Northumbria Police* (CA 1996) it was held that the immunity could be displaced by other more compelling circumstances. In this case, the plaintiff supplied confidential information to the police about a serious crime, naming a person who, to police knowledge, was violent. As a result of police negligence that information fell into the hands of the person named and the plaintiff suffered subsequent psychiatric injury in consequence of the threats made against him.

It was held that the Police could hold a duty of care in these circumstances.

Rescue services

The Court of Appeal has ruled that there is no proximity of relationship between the fire brigade and a building owner. Fire brigades are not under a common law duty of care to answer an emergency call nor under a duty to take reasonable care to do so. Unless the fire brigade negligently increased the likelihood of the fire such a duty will not arise.

Public bodies

In respect of local authorities, in the case of *X (Minors) v Bedfordshire County Council* (HL 1995) the House of Lords ruled that there is no duty of care on local authorities in carrying out their discretionary statutory functions. However, where conduct results from an improper exercise of that discretion liability can arise.

Negligence-breach of duty

Once it has been established that a duty of care is owed to a claimant, it must then be proven that the defendant was in breach of that duty.

The key definition of negligence and duty of care was defined in *Blythe v Birmingham Waterworks* Co (1856). In this case, a wooden plug in a water main became loose in a severe frost. The plug led to a pipe which in turn went up the street. However, this pipe was blocked with ice, and the water instead flooded the claimant's house. The claimant sued in negligence. In this case, Alderson B defined negligence as:

"the omission to do something which a reasonable man, guided upon those considerations which ordinarily regulate the conduct of human affairs, would do, or doing something which a prudent and reasonable man would not do".

The key word here is *"reasonable man"*. The standard of care required of the defendant is that of the hypothetical reasonable man. This standard is objective as it does not take into account particular traits of an individual. In *Hall v Brooklands Auto Racing Club* (1933) Greer LJ described such a person as:

- the 'man in the street'; or
- 'the man on the Clapham Omnibus; or
- 'the man who takes the magazines at home, and in the evening pushes the lawnmower in his shirt sleeves'

The reasonable person is therefore an 'average' person and not perfect. The standard of reasonable care is invariable in the sense that the law does not recognise differing degrees of negligence but it is an infinitely flexible concept enabling the court in any given situation to impose standards ranging from high to low.

What is reasonable conduct varies with the particular circumstance, and liability depends ultimately what the reasonable man would have foreseen, which in turn may depend upon what particular knowledge and experience, if any, is to be attributed to him. However, although a defendant is not negligent if the consequences of his conduct were unforeseeable, it does not necessarily follow that the defendant will be responsible for all foreseeable consequences. In practice the courts evaluate a defendant's behaviour in terms of risk, so that he will be seen to be negligent if the claimant is exposed to an unreasonable risk of harm.

Other notable cases of alleged breach of duty include:

Condon v Basi [1985]
During a football match the Claimant suffered a broken leg after a challenge from the defendant. Both clubs involved were in the Leamington Local League. The Court's question was as to the standard of care expected from a football player.

The Court held that the standard of care varies according to the level of expertise of the player. The Defendant was in breach of duty as the tackle was considered reckless.

Blake v Galloway [2004]

The Claimant (a fifteen year old boy), was with friends when he threw a piece of tree bark at his friend's leg, the friend then threw the bark back at him, which consequently hit him in the eye causing serious injury. The Claimant contended that the injury was brought about by the negligence of the Defendant. The *volenti non fit injuria* defence was then raised by the Defendant however this was rejected and the judge held that the damages should be reduced by 50%.

Hilsher v Essex [1988]

A premature baby was given too much oxygen by a junior doctor. The baby was found to suffer from a condition damaging his retina which left him completely blind in one eye and partially sighted in the other. The excess oxygen could have been the cause of the impairment of his retina however other factors relating to the premature birth also could have been the cause. The judge found the Health Authority liable for negligence.

Nettleship v Weston [1971]

The Defendant was a learner driver. She was taking lessons from a friend who checked that the Defendant's insurance covered for her to be a passenger in the car. During a trip in the car the Defendant hit a lamp post and subsequently fractured the Claimant's knee. The Defendant raised that as a learner driver her responsibility for standard of care should be lowered however this was not held but damages were reduced by 50%.

Special standards of care

There are certain situations in which the courts will apply a different standard of care from that of the 'reasonable' person:

- Where the defendant has a particular skill
- where the defendant has a particular lack of skill
- Where the defendant is a child
- Where the defendant is competing in or watching a sporting event.

Skilled or professional defendants

The standard of care applied to professional with a particular skill or expertise is that of the reasonable person with the same skill or expertise. For example a doctor would be expected to show a greater degree of skill and care to a patient than 'the man on the Clapham omnibus'. See below.

Magnitude of the risk

The degree of care which the law expects must be commensurate with the risk created. Two factors are involved, namely the likelihood that harm will be caused and the potential gravity of that harm. In the case *Bolton v Stone* (HL 1951) the plaintiff was standing in the road when she was struck by a cricket ball which had been hit out of the defendants ground. There was some evidence that this had happened before on an infrequent basis, i.e. six times in thirty years, so that the risk was one of which the defendants were aware and which was reasonably foreseeable. However, the defendants were not held liable because the risk was so small that they were perfectly justified in not taking any further measures to eliminate that risk.

Another case illustrating magnitude and gravity of the risk is that of *Paris v Stepney B.C* (HL 1951) where a person with one eye, a garage worker, became totally blind after being struck in the eye by a metal chip which flew from a bolt which he was trying to hammer loose. The defendants, his employers, were held liable for failing to provide him with safety goggles, even though they were justified in not providing such equipment to a person with normal sight. Although the risk was small, the injury to this particular person was very serious.

Another case which illustrates the magnitude of risk is that of *Watson v British Boxing Board of Control* (2001) where the board breached its duty in failing to inform itself adequately about the risks inherent to a blow to the head and by failing to provide resuscitation equipment to be provided at the ringside together with persons able to operate it.

The degree of risk to which a claimant is exposed will also depend upon any physical abnormality from which he may suffer so that, if such abnormality is or ought to be known to the defendant, that is a factor which should be taken into account.

Characteristics of the defendant

The general legal standard does not take into account the personal characteristics of a particular defendant. Inexperience, lack of intelligence or other provide no defence to negligence. For example, a partially sighted driver owes the same level of duty as a normally sighted driver. However, two types of defendant require mention.

Children

As far as children are concerned, there is no defence of minority as such and a child is responsible for its torts, through its guardian *ad litem*. For example, In the case *Gorely v Codd* (HC 1967) a boy of 16 was held to be negligent in the use of an air rifle. However, as in cases of contributory negligence, it was held in *Mullin v Richards* (CA 1998) that the standard of care is that which can reasonably expected of an ordinary child of the defendant's age. In this case, two fifteen year old schoolgirls were fencing with plastic rulers during a class when one of the rulers snapped and a fragment of plastic caused one of them to damage her eye. Where a young child does cause injury through negligence by conduct which an adult would be classed as negligent then the parents would be responsible for its actions. This is a primary liability arising from a failure to exercise proper supervision and control.

Professionals

Professionals must attain the standard of the reasonably competent person exercising that skill or profession. The level of skill demanded, however, will vary according to the extent of the risk. A member of a profession discharges their duty by conforming to the standards of a reasonably competent member of that profession and inexperience is no excuse. For example, a doctor must act in accordance with a practice accepted as proper by a body of responsible and skilled medical opinion, and is not negligent merely because there is a body of opinion which would take a contrary view. This was the test laid down in *Bolam v Friern Barnet Hospital Management Committee* (HC 1957). In this case the claimant underwent a course of electro-convulsive therapy in hospital as treatment for severe depression. Given the nature of this procedure, and the risks involved, great care is needed. The doctor failed to provide the claimant with any muscle relaxants or any physical restraints and the claimant suffered a dislocation of both hip joints with fractures of the pelvis on each side. The court had to decide whether it was negligent not to provide relaxants or restraints. The main legal principle to arise was that the standard of care for doctors is the 'standard of care of the ordinary skilled man exercising and professing to have that special skill'.

An error of judgement by a professional may or may not be negligent, depending upon whether it was such as a reasonably competent practitioner would make. This was illustrated in the case of *Whitehouse v Jordan* (HL 1981). It is, however, part of the duty of the professional to keep abreast of new developments and techniques, as what is reasonably foreseeable may depend on the state of existing knowledge within that profession at the time.

Evidence of negligence

It is for the claimant to prove, on a balance of probabilities, that the defendant was negligent. This is subject to the proviso contained within the Civil Evidence Act 1968 s.11, that proof that a person stands convicted of an offence is conclusive evidence in civil proceedings that he did commit it unless the contrary is proved. The effect of this provision is to shift the burden of proof where the claimant proves that the defendant has been convicted of an offence involving conduct complained of as negligent, such as careless driving.

In order to discharge the burden of proof the claimant must usually prove particular conduct on the part of the defendant which can be regarded as negligent. The claimant will not be able to do so, however, if he does not know how the accident was caused and, in such a case, the maxim *res ipsa loquitur* (the thing speaks for itself) may be relied on.

This is a rule of evidence that the claimant, who is unable to explain how the accident happened, asks the court to make a *prima facie* finding of negligence, which it is then for the defendant to rebut if he or she can. There are three conditions necessary for the application of the doctrine which arose out of *Scott v London and St Katherines Docks Co (EC 1865)*: there must be an absence of an explanation as to how the accident happened, the 'thing' which causes the damage must be under control of the defendant (or someone for whose negligence he is responsible) and the accident must be such as would not ordinarily occur without negligence.

Notes on medical negligence and COVID 19

In time some patients may feel that they or their loved ones were treated improperly, negligently during the crisis and seek redress, raising the spectre of litigation. NHS staff may also feel prompted to sue their employers for failing to take reasonable care to ensure their health and safety at work. Such legal claims would be complicated and there are established legal principles decided over many years which could help frame actions if they are decided on.

The extra demand and pressure placed on the NHS because of the COVID-19 outbreak has led to emergency measures within the health service. Retired doctors have been called back into service, while final year medical students have started work early and in primary and secondary care, doctors are working outside their areas of expertise.

Taking this emergency response into account, the Medical Defence Union (MDU) says doctors should be spared from the stress and anxiety of medical negligence claims following the pandemic.

The organisation, which provides legal support to doctors, nurses, dentists, and other healthcare workers, has raised concerns that; "*medical liability claims will come long after public memory of the sacrifices made by healthcare workers have been forgotten and the circumstances of the pandemic which requires people to work outside their speciality and beyond their experience will also be forgotten.*"

The organisation's concerns echo wider national newspaper reports. One such report states the "*NHS could be faced with billions of pounds of medical negligence claims if it does not grant some form of legal immunity to medics risking their lives during the pandemic, the government has been warned*".

The MDU's viewpoint also references that several states in the US have implemented laws that provide healthcare professionals and hospitals with "*immunity from civil liability for any injury or death alleged to have been sustained because of any acts or omissions undertaken in good faith*".

While it can seem logical to be empathetic to such proposed measures of immunity, taking this approach does raise the question about patient safety. It could be construed that healthcare professionals made fatal mistakes because of the conditions of an emergency or extreme situation. Errors would be effectively excused by good intentions, meaning the importance of patient safety is ignored.

Granting immunity to medical liabilities during the pandemic could also cast doubt on patient safety in the future. Although the pandemic is unprecedented, medical professionals may also find themselves in other emergencies, where they are faced with uncertainties. In such instances, would doctors and nurses be able to claim immunity because they weren't familiar with the circumstances, which they found themselves in?

Before calling for immunity, it is also worth considering that only a very small minority of potential medical claims will reach the MDU or NHS Resolutions (who deal with claims against the NHS) and then it still needs to be established that the care was negligent. This is done by demonstrating the following:

1. It has to be established that the standard of treatment provided has fallen below the standard expected of a reasonably competent doctor dealing with the patient's particular condition. Put simply, if a patient was in a room with a number of doctors practicing in the same area as a doctor deemed to have acted negligently, there would have to be general consensus amongst the other doctors that each of them would have acted differently during the patient's treatment, for any level of negligence to be considered.

2. If it can be established the treatment was below standard, the claimant would then have to show that the poor treatment has caused extra pain, suffering, loss and damage over and above that which they may

have experienced even if they had received the appropriate treatment.

3. This process is very onerous on a potential claimant.

4. The debate around immunity should also consider other steps that are being taken during the pandemic. The government has promised to cover the cost of any future legal actions by providing indemnities and a new scheme, Clinical Negligence Scheme for Coronavirus (CNSC), has already been launched by NHS Resolution to indemnify healthcare professionals for any clinical liabilities arising from the pandemic and has been established under the Coronavirus Act 2020. It has been designed to provide cover for the *"new contracts being put in place for healthcare arrangements to respond to coronavirus such as those with the Independent Sector and organisations supporting testing arrangements"*.

In its announcement, the MDU admits that doctors should be accountable for their actions and confirmed that the General Medical Council (GMC) has already recognised that different considerations will need to be applied when investigating complaints. Given the circumstances of the pandemic, this seems a more constructive course of action for both patients and medical professionals and raises less question of patient safety being disregarded because of an emergency situation.

****

Ch. 2

Negligence-Causation and Remoteness of Damage

Causation and remoteness provide the crucial link between the defendant's negligent conduct and the harm suffered by the claimant.

The previous chapter covered duty of care whilst in this chapter we will look at causation and remoteness of damage.

The issues of causation and remoteness relate to the law of tort generally but are dealt with in the context of negligence. Most of the problems have arisen within this context. Unless the claimant can prove that the defendant's tort caused the loss suffered by him then the action will fail, or in the case of torts actionable per se, only nominal damages will be recovered. Even if the claimant can prove a causal connection the claim may still fail if the damage is too remote.

Causation

It must first be established that the breach was the cause of the damage, or materially contributed to the damage. In determining this issue, it is usual to employ the 'but for' test, the function of which is to eliminate those factors which could not have had any causal effect. One case which illustrates this is *Cork v Kirby Maclean 1952* Where a workman, an epileptic, was set to work painting the roof inside a factory, which necessitated his doing the work from a platform some 23 feet above the floor of the factory. The platform was some 27 inches wide and was used for the deposit of the workman's brush and bucket. There were no guard-rails or toe boards. The workman fell from the platform and was killed. In this case, Lord Denning stated:

...if the damage would not have happened but for a particular fault, then that fault is the cause of the damage; if it would have happened just the same, fault or no fault, the fault is not the cause of the damage.

Another case is *Barnett v Chelsea and Kensington Hospital Management Committee* (HC 1969) where the failure of a casualty officer to examine a patient, who subsequently died of arsenic poisoning, was held not to have been a cause of death because evidence showed that the patient would have probably died in any event.

Difficulties may arise where the precise cause of the damage is unknown. In *McGhee v National Coal Board* (HL 1972) the patient contracted dermatitis as a result of exposure to abrasive dust at work. His employers were not at fault for the exposure during the normal course of his work, but were found to be negligent for failing to provide washing facilities with the result that he was caked in dust for longer than necessary as he cycled home. The plaintiff succeeded on the ground that it was sufficient to show that the defendant's breach materially increased the risk of injury, even though medical knowledge at the time was unable to establish the breach as the probable cause. This decision had far reaching effects, particularly in cases of medical negligence.

An attempt was made in *Hotson v East Berkshire Area Health Authority* (HL 1987) to extend the principle so as to impose a liability in respect of the loss of a chance of recovery. In this case, the plaintiff injured his hip in a fall and, as a result of negligent medical diagnosis, suffered a permanent deformity the risk of which would have been reduced by 25 per cent had the proper treatment been given at the time. The Court of Appeal upheld the finding but this was overturned by the House of Lords on the grounds that there was no principle in law which would have justified a discount from the full measure of damages.

In cases where successive acts cause damage, the position is more complex. In *Baker v Willoughby* (HL 1970) the plaintiff's leg was injured through the defendant's negligence, and some time later, before the trial, he was shot in the same leg during a robbery. The leg was then amputated. It was held in this case that the plaintiff's right of recovery was not limited to the loss suffered only before the date of the robbery, but that he was entitled to damages that he would have received had there been no subsequent injury.

In another case, *Jobling v Associated Dairies Limited* (HL 1980) the defendant's negligence caused a reduction in the plaintiffs earning capacity. Three years later, but before the trial, the defendant was found to be suffering from another complaint, wholly unrelated to the original accident, which totally incapacitated him. The defendant's were held liable only for the loss up to the time of the plaintiff's disablement.

Other notable causation cases

Chester v Afshar (2004)

The Claimant suffered back pain for 6 years which became severe to the point at times she was unable to control her bladder or walk. After an MRI scan it was revealed that there was a disk protrusion into the spinal column and she was therefore advised to have surgery. The surgery carried a 1-2% risk that the procedure could worsen the Claimant's back pain further. Her consultant, Mr Afshar, failed to warn of the risks of the surgery. The Claimant submitted that if she knew of the risk she may not have gone ahead with the surgery and would have at least taken more time to consider her decision. The judge held that there was a possibility on another occasion the surgery may have been successful, therefore he found for the Claimant.

Performance Cars Ltd v Abraham (1962)

The Claimant's car, a silver Rolls Royce, was hit by the Defendant who admitted to breach of duty. Two weeks prior to this incident the Claimant had been in a previous incident with another negligent driver. The Claimant claimed for a respray of the car (£75) however, the Claimant was yet to receive the sum. The Claimant then tried to claim for the second incident however it was conceded the Claimant could not recover the same loss twice. The judge held the first defendant was responsible for the whole amount therefore the Defendant was absolved from liability to pay.

Bonnington Castings Ltd v Wardlaw (1956)

During the course of his employment the Claimant developed pneumoconiosis by inhaling air which contained minute

45

particles of silica. The Defendant was in breach of statutory duty in failing to provide an extractor fan. If the extractor fan had been installed the Claimant would have been exposed to fewer silica particles in the air. The Defendant was unable to prove that the Claimant would have developed pneumoconiosis even if the fan was installed therefore the Defendant was held liable.

Fitzgerald v Lane (1989)

The Claimant walked across a pelican crossing when the lights were red when he was hit by the First Defendant and fell into the path of the Second Defendant. He consequentially suffered from tetraplegia, however was unable to confirm which impact caused the tetraplegia. The judge held that all three were equally at fault with both defendants paying insufficient attention to the road. Damages were held at £596,553 and ordered the two Defendants to pay one third of that amount.

Remoteness of damage

The plaintiff is not entitled to compensation for every consequence of the defendant's wrong. In order to contain the defendant's liability within reasonable bounds, a line is drawn, and the consequences that fall on the far side of the line are said to be too remote and not having been caused in law by the defendant's breach of duty.

There are a number of cases which have provided tests of remoteness of damage. In *Re Polemis and Furness, Withy and Co* (CA 1921) a ship's cargo of benzene had leaked filling the hold with inflammable vapour. Stevedores unloading the vessel negligently dropped a plank in the hold, and the defendant employers were held liable for the destruction of the ship in the blaze that followed because that loss was a direct, although unforeseeable consequence of the negligence.

Whilst not denying the relevance of foreseeability to the existence of a duty, the case did decide that it was not relevant in determining for what consequences the defendant should pay.

However, in another case, *Overseas Tankship (UK) Ltd v Morts Dock Engineering Co Ltd (The Wagon Mound)*, 1961 this approach was disproved. A test of reasonable foresight of consequence was substituted for that of directness. The defendants, in this case, negligently discharged into Sydney Harbour a large quantity of fuel oil which drifted to the plaintiff's wharf whilst welding was in progress. The plaintiff's discontinued their operations, but later resumed following an assurance that there was no danger of the oil igniting. A fire did eventually break out, causing damage to the wharf and to two ships upon which work was being carried out. It was found as a fact that some damage to the wharf was reasonably foreseeable by way of fouling the slipway, but that, in view of expert evidence, it was unforeseeable that the oil would ignite. The defendant's were, accordingly, held not liable.

Manner of occurrence

In *Hughes v Lord Advocate* (HL 1963) post office employees negligently left a manhole uncovered with a canvas shelter over it, surrounded by paraffin lamps. The plaintiff, aged eight, took none of the lamps into the shelter and knocked it into the manhole. There was an explosion, following an unusual combination of circumstances, in which the boy was badly burned. Although the explosion was unforeseeable, the defendants were held liable because burns from the lamp were foreseeable, and it was immaterial that the precise chain of events leading to the injury was not.

A contrasting case is that of *Doughty v Turner Manufacturing Co Ltd* (CA 1964) in which the defendant's employee dropped an asbestos cover into a vat of molten liquid which, due to an unforeseeable chemical reaction, erupted and burned a fellow worker standing nearby. It was held that, even if injury by splashing were foreseeable the eruption was not, and the plaintiff failed. This case is at odds with Hughes (above) because if it accepted that some injury by burning was foreseeable, then it ought not to matter that the way in which it occurred was not.

Type of damage

The exact nature of the damage need not be foreseeable, provided it is of a type that could have been foreseen. The difficulty here, of defining damage 'of a type' is illustrated by two contrasting cases. The first case, *Bradford v Robinson Rentals Ltd* (HC 1967) a van driver sent on a long journey in an unheated vehicle in severe weather was able to recover damages for frostbite because, although not in itself foreseeable, it was in the broad class of foreseeable risk arising from exposure to severe cold.

The second case, *Tremain v Pike* (HC 1969) the defendant's alleged negligence caused his farm to become rat-infested with the result that the plaintiff contracted a rare disease by contact with rats urine. It was held that, even if negligence had been proved, the plaintiff could not succeed because although injury from rat bites or food contamination was foreseeable, this particularly rare disease was entirely different in kind.

Extent of damage

When considering the extent of damage, it doesn't matter that the actual damage is far greater in extent than could have been foreseen. In *Vacwell Engineering Co Ltd v B.D.H. Chemicals Ltd* (CA 1971) the plaintiffs purchased a chemical manufactured and supplied by the defendants, who failed to give warning that it was liable to cause a minor explosion on contact with water. The plaintiff's employee placed a large amount of the chemical in a sink and an explosion of unforeseeable violence badly damaged the premises. Since the explosion and subsequent damage were foreseeable, even though the extent was not, the defendants were held liable.

A similar rule operates where the claimant suffers foreseeable personal injury which is exacerbated by some pre-existing physical or psychic abnormality. This so called "egg-shell skull" principle imposes liability on the defendant for harm which is not only greater in extent than, but which is of an entirely different kind to, that which is foreseeable. In *Smith v Leech Brain and Co Ltd* (HC 1962) a workman who had a predisposition to cancer received a burn on the lip from molten metal due to a colleague's negligence. The defendants were held liable for his subsequent death from cancer triggered by the burn.

The principle applies equally to a claimant who suffers from nervous shock. In *Meah v McCreamer* (HC 1985) the plaintiff underwent a marked personality change brought about by injuries received in a collision for which the defendant was responsible. This led him to commit a series of assaults for which he received a life sentence. He recovered damages for loss of liberty.

Intervening causes

In some cases, the claimant's damage is alleged to be attributable not to the defendant's breach of duty, but to some intervening event which breaks the chain of causation. Such an event is called a *novus actus interveniens* and is usually dealt with as part of the issue of remoteness because even though the damage would not have occurred "but for" the defendants breach, it may still be regarded in law as falling outside the scope of the risk created by the original fault.

One such case that illustrates this is *McKew v Holland* and *Hannen and Cubitts* (Scotland) Ltd (HL 1969) where the plaintiff's leg occasionally gave way without warning as a result of the defendant's negligence. On one such occasion he fractured his ankle as a result of descending a flight of stairs where his leg gave way.

The defendant's were held not liable for this further injury because, although foreseeable, the plaintiff's conduct was *so* unreasonable as to amount to a *novus actus*. However, each case on its own merit.

Whether the issue is seen as *novus actus* or of contributory negligence (which is the more common approach) will depend upon the nature of the plaintiff's conduct and it may be that a positive act is more likely to break the causal chain than a mere omission.

Intervention of a third party

According to Lord Reid in *Dorset Yacht Co Ltd v Home Office* (HL 1970) the intervention of a third party must have been something very likely to happen if it is not regarded as breaking the chain of causation. The question is what is the potential liability of a defendant for the criminal act of another? In the case *Knightly v Johns* (CA 1982) the defendant negligently caused a crash on a dangerous bend in a one-way tunnel. The police inspector at the scene of the accident forgot to close the tunnel to oncoming traffic as he ought to have done in accordance with standing orders, so he ordered the plaintiff officer to ride back on his motorcycle against the flow of traffic in order to do so, and the plaintiff was injured in a further collision. It was said that, in considering whether the intervening act of a third party breaks the chain of causation, the test is whether the damage is reasonably foreseeable in the sense of being a 'natural and probable' result of the defendant's breach. A deliberate decision to do a positive act is more likely to break the chain than a mere omission. In this case, the inspector's errors amounted to tortuous negligence which cannot be described as the natural and probable consequence of the original collision, and the defendant was held not liable.

Intervening natural force

The defendant will not normally be held liable for damage suffered as the immediate consequence of a natural event which occurs independently of the breach. In the case *Carslogie Steamship Co Ltd v Royal Norwegian Government* (HL 1952) the defendants were held not liable for storm damage suffered by a ship during a voyage to a place where repairs to collision damage caused by the defendant's negligence were to be done, even though that voyage would not have been undertaken had the collision not occurred.

Ch. 3

Contributory Negligence

To succeed in this defence, it is not necessary for the defendant to prove that the claimant owed a duty of care but simply that the claimant contributed through lack of reasonable care.

Since the passage of the Law Reform (Contributory Negligence) Act 1945 contributory negligence is no longer a complete bar to recovery but, in accordance with s.1(1) of the act, will result in a reduction of damages to such an extent as is seen as just and equitable.

The Act applies where the damage is attributable to the fault of both parties, and 'fault' is defined in section 4 to mean "negligence, breach of statutory duty, or other act or omission which gives rise to a liability in tort or would, apart from this act, give rise to the defence of contributory negligence". The defence, therefore, applies to actions other than negligence, though it does not apply to deceit or intentional interference with goods - Torts (Interference With Goods) Act 1977 s.11).

Causation

The damage suffered must be caused partly by the fault of the claimant and it is therefore irrelevant that the claimant's fault was nothing to do with the accident. Thus, reductions in damages have been made for failure to wear a seat belt or a crash helmet and for travelling in a vehicle with a drunk driver.

One case which highlights this is *Jones v Livox Quarries Ltd (CA 1952)*. The plaintiff, contrary to instructions, stood on a rear towbar of a vehicle and was injured when another vehicle ran into the back of it. In this case, damages were reduced as the claimant had exposed himself to risk. The claimant is expected to show an objective standard of care in much the same way as the defendant must to avoid tortuous negligence.

There are particular cases in contributory negligence, children, old or infirm persons and rescuers merit special attention.

Children

As a matter of law thee is no age below which it can be said that a child is incapable of contributory negligence. However, the degree of care expected must be apportioned to the age of the child.

For example, in *Gough v Thorne (CA 1966)* a 13 year old girl who was knocked down by a negligent motorist when she stepped past a stationary lorry whose driver had beckoned her to cross, was held not guilty of contributory negligence. However, in *Morales v Eccleston* (CA 1991) an 11 year old boy who was struck by the defendant driver while kicking a ball in the middle of the road with traffic passing in either direction had his damages reduced by 75 per cent.

An important case in this respects is the case of Master Caine Ellis v Mr Paul Kelly and Mrs Violet Ellis on 31 July 2018. It is worth outlining this case in full.

Caine was involved in a road traffic accident on 20 September 2008, when he was 8 years old. He had been struck by Mr Kelly's car whilst crossing a road close to his home. He suffered a traumatic brain injury and is unlikely to be able to live interpedently or undertake any kind of paid employment. That is as far as the Judgment commented on the value of the claim. Primary liability was admitted and the live issues at trial were firstly, whether Caine should be found contributory negligent for his part in the accident and secondly, whether his mother, Violet Ellis, should bear any responsibility.

The Facts

Caine comes from a close family. His mother, allowed him to him to go out to the local park without adult supervision if he was accompanied by one of his older cousins, who were 10 and 11 years old respectively. When they were out, the children were encouraged to stay together, and they had a mobile phone with them, so they could keep in contact with their parents in case of an emergency.

Caine's mother had taught him the Green Cross Code as she walked him to school and everywhere else. She did not allow him to go out without an adult until she thought it was safe.

On the day of the accident, Caine had gone to the park with his 11-year old cousin, Cyrus. After they had been in the park for some time, Cyrus had left to attend a skate park nearby, leaving Caine with his 10-year old cousin, Chloe. A short while later, Caine wanted to go to the skate park as well and eventually left the park by himself to find Cyrus.

It is not completely clear what happened next, but Caine did not find Cyrus at the skate park. It is suspected that he went to the local shop on Gospel Lane to attempt to find him. Caine ran into Gospel Road in a diagonal direction towards a zebra crossing. As he ran into the road, he was struck by Mr Kelly's vehicle.

Lay witness evidence suggested that Mr Kelly was driving in excess of the 30mph speed limit. The accident reconstruction experts called by the Caine's legal team and Insurers reached an agreed view that he was driving at between 31mph and 40mph. They also agreed that if Mr Kelly had been driving at 30mph he would have been able to stop safely and avoid the collision.

Contributory Negligence

The insurers' argument on this issue, was that Caine was negligent as he ran into the road when Mr Kelly's vehicle was near him and a clear danger. They also alleged that he ran out from a position which gave Mr Kelly a limited opportunity to react.

Mrs Justice Yip set out the legal basis for determining whether a party had been contributory negligent. The Law Reform (Contributory Negligence) Act 1945 states:

"Where any person suffers damage as the result partly of his own fault and party of the fault of any other person, a claim in respect of that damage shall not be defeated by reason of the fault of the person suffering the damage, but the damages recoverable in respect thereof shall be reduced to such extent as the court thinks just and equitable having regard to the claimant's share in the responsibility for the damage".

Lord Denning applied this test in the case of Davies v Swan Motor Co Ltd (1949). Mrs Justice Yip confirmed that it is now very well established that apportioning responsibility between a claimant and defendant involved a consideration of the causative potency of what they have done and their relative blameworthiness.

Mrs Justice Yip stated that the was "no hard and fast rule" as to which age a child could be found   could be found contributory negligent. In judging the actions of a child, the standard of care is to be measured by that reasonably to be expected of a child of the same age, intelligence and experience.

The insurers relied on the case of AB v Main 2015 EWHC 3183(QB) where child aged 8 years and 10 months was found to be 20% contributory negligent. The driver in that case was found to be driving 10mph under the speed limit. The insurers did not rely on any other cases involving a successful finding of negligence against an 8-year old. Mrs Justice Yip stated that a finding against a child of that age was uncommon.

Accordingly, any finding of contributory negligence will be determined by the facts of the case. Irrespective of the admission of primary liability, Mrs Justice Yip first considered Mr Kelly's blameworthiness. She found that he was clearly driving faster than the 30mph speed limit. She also found that Gospel Road was well known to be a play area, with lots of children around. She considered that irrespective of the speed limit, a safe speed on Gospel Road was no more than 20mph.

She found that Caine's experience of Gospel Road was likely that it was a safe place to be, as drivers normally drove along there with caution. It was to his great misfortune that the first time he crossed it alone, he was faced with a car being driven in a way he had never experienced before i.e. at excess speed and with no consideration for children playing close by.

Mrs Justice Yip contrasted Mr Kelly's blameworthiness and the causative potency of his actions against Caine's actions. She stated the following whilst dismissing the insurers' submissions for a finding of contributory negligence

"I find that this was a case of momentary misjudgement on Caine's part balanced against reckless conduct of the part of the defendant, whose driving was outside Caine's expectations based on his understanding an experience. In my judgment it would not be just and equitable to make a finding of contributory negligence in these circumstances and I decline to do so."

Mrs Ellis' Liability

The insurers did not pursue an argument that Caine's mother was negligent in allowing him to go out with his older cousins. Their allegation of negligence was based on a perceived failure to provide Caine with clear and detailed rules about what should happen whilst he was out with his cousins.

The insurers only confirmed at trial that they were not seeking a contribution from Mrs Ellis towards Caine's damages and legal costs. They were raising only the argument to attack her gratuitous care claim for the assistance she now had to provide to Caine.

Mrs Justice Yip's opening comment after dismissing the Part 20 was that she found that Mrs Ellis was a responsible mother who took proper care for her son. She also stated the following:

"No matter how careful a parent is, it is impossible for children to be completely protected from risk. Keeping children cooped up and not allowing them to experiment with small freedoms carries its own risk. There is a difficult balance to be

struck. Different parents in different circumstances will make different decisions about how best to strike that balance. Sadly, when something goes catastrophically wrong, a parent may look back and agonise over the choice they made. The fact that, with hindsight, they would have taken a different course is very far from establishing that their original choice was wrong, still less that they were negligent."

She found that holding Mrs Ellis responsible would be to impose far too high a standard on an ordinary parent making ordinary decisions during parenting as to how to keep their child reasonably safe.

She did not agree with the insurers' submission that it would unreasonable for a child to be held too young to be held contributory negligent but for the parent not to be liable for allowing them to be out alone and stated the following:

"Each party's responsibility is to be considered separately by reference to the appropriate standard of care. In the case of the child, this is the standard of a reasonable child of his age and understanding. In the case of the parent, it is the standard of a reasonable parent. I have explained why, in the circumstances of this case, I do not consider Caine or Mrs Ellis to have fallen below the relevant standard such that responsibility should attach to either of them."

Old or infirm persons

When assessing whether such a person is guilty of contributory negligence, the age and infirmity and its impact on the alleged negligence is taken into account.

Rescuers

It is not very often, for obvious reasons, that a rescuer will be found guilty of contributory negligence. In *Brandon v Osborne, Garret and Co Ltd* (HC 1924) the defendants negligently allowed a sheet of glass to fall from their shop roof and the plaintiff, believing her husband to be in danger, tried to pull him away and injured her leg. She was held to not be contributorily negligent. A similar principle applies where the claimant is injured in trying to extricate himself or herself from a perilous situation in which the defendants negligence has placed them, even though, with hindsight the claimant is shown to have chosen the wrong course of action. As with all such cases, each case is viewed on its own merit.

Apportionment

Apportionment is on a just and equitable basis according to the 1945 Act and, in assessing the claimant's reduction, the court may take into account both the potency of his act and the degree of blameworthiness to be attached to it. The Court of Appeal has held, in *Johnson v Tennant Bros Ltd* (CA 1954) that no apportionment should be made unless one of the parties is at least 10 per cent to blame. However, the decisions concerning apportionment is left, mainly, to judicial discretion.

Violenti Non Fit Injuria

This maxim embodies a principle that a person who expressly or impliedly agrees with another to run the risk of harm created by that other person cannot then sue in respect of damage suffered as a result of the materialisation of that risk.

The defence is called consent or voluntary assumption of risk and, if successful, is a complete bar to recovery.

For the defence to apply the defendant must have committed what would, in the absence of any consent, amount to a tort. The defendant must prove not only that the claimant consented to the risk of actual damage, but also that he or she agreed to waive their right of action in respect of that damage.

Knowledge of the risk

Knowledge of the risk does not amount to consent. It must be found that the claimant, with full knowledge of the risk, agreed to incur it.

Agreement

In relation to agreement, in addition to the claimant being willing to take the risk, there must be evidence that the claimant has expressly or impliedly agreed to waive his or her course of action. An express antecedent agreement to relieve the defendant of liability for future negligence operates in effect as an exclusion notice and is therefore subject to the Unfair Contract terms Act 1977. Section 2(1) renders void any purported exclusion of liability for death or personal injury caused by negligence and, in the case of other loss or damage, s.2(2) subjects such an exclusion to a test of reasonableness. Section 2(3) further provides that a persons agreement to, or awareness of, such a notice is not of itself to be taken as indicating his voluntary acceptance of any risk. These provisions only apply to business liability.

In some circumstances the conduct of the parties may enable an inference to be drawn that the claimant has impliedly agreed to waive his legal rights in respect of future negligence. One such case was *Morris v Murray* (CA 1990). The defence applied when, in poor weather conditions, the defendant, who to the plaintiff's knowledge was extremely drunk, took the plaintiff for a spin and crashed the aircraft immediately after takeoff.

With negligence cases in the sporting arena, the potential liability of the participant depends upon the standard of care owed. In any sporting event, the spectator may be taken to have accepted the risks incidental to the game, for example, being hit by a cricket ball whilst watching a game of cricket. In the case *Wooldridge v Sumner* (CA 1963) it was stated that sportsmen and women have a duty not to behave with reckless disregard for the spectator. This applies to the duty of care required between one player and another. In *Watson v British Boxing Board of Control* (2001) it was pointed out that where the plaintiff consents to injury by an opponent in a boxing ring he does not consent to injury resulting from inadequate safety arrangements by the sports governing body after being hit.

Car passengers

A passenger who accepts a lift with a driver whose ability to drive is impaired, for example by drink, cannot be held *volenti* to the risk, because section 149 of the Road Traffic Act 1988 prohibits any restriction on the drivers ability to his passenger as is required to be covered by insurance. Taking a lift with an drunk driver is, however, likely to amount to contributory negligence.

In Froom v Butcher [1976] QB 286, the driver of a vehicle was not wearing his seatbelt and suffered head and chest injuries in a collision caused by the Defendant's negligence. Lord Denning in the Court of Appeal stated that *"whenever there is an accident, the negligent driver must bear by far the greater share of responsibility."* But where the evidence showed that, had a seat belt been worn, injury would have been avoided altogether, it was appropriate to reduce damages by 25% for the negligence of the injured person in failing to wear the seatbelt – where the wearing of the seatbelt would not have avoided injury altogether but the injuries would have been considerably reduced, the appropriate deduction might be 15%.

At the time of Froom v Butcher, it was not a criminal offence to fail to wear a seatbelt, although Lord Denning referred to the information available through the press and other sources as to the risks inherent in not wearing seat belts and to fact that legislation was being contemplated to make the wearing of seatbelts compulsory.

In a more recent case in the High Court before Cox J, Stanton v Collinson [2009] EWHC 342, the issue was considered yet again. The Claimant and another passenger sat in the front seat of a car driven by the deceased, neither wearing a seat belt. The deceased lost control of the vehicle at speed, causing an accident in which he was killed and the Claimant (amongst others) was injured. Primary liability was admitted on behalf of the estate of the deceased.

The Judge considered the Claimant's argument that the Defendant had not shown that, even if the Claimant had been wearing a seatbelt, his injuries would have been any less. The Claimant suffered a serious head injury in the accident causing brain injury. The joint statement of engineering experts agreed that the severity of the head injury would have been reduced had the Claimant been wearing a seatbelt, but complete prevention of head injury would have been unlikely.

The Defendant did not call any medical evidence as to the effects of a less severe head injury and the Judge concluded that the Defendant had not discharged the burden of proving that the Claimant's action in not wearing a seat belt was causative of his injuries. Accordingly the Claimant recovered in full.

Rescuers

If the defendant's negligence endangers the safety of others such that a rescue attempt is reasonably foreseeable, a duty is owed to the rescuer. It makes no difference that the person imperilled is actually the defendant is actually the defendant rather than the third party and the duty owed is wholly independent of any duty owed by the defendant to those who are rescued. Nor is there any rule of law to prevent a claim by a professional 'rescuer' so that a fireman injured whilst fighting a negligently started fire may recover damages.

In the case *Chadwick v British Transport Commission* (HC 1967) a rescuer who assisted at the scene of a train crash and who suffered nervous shock as a result of what he saw was held entitled to recover damages, even though he was in no personal danger.

Ex Turpi Causa

Where an alleged wrong occurs whilst the claimant is engaged in criminal activity, the claim may be barred because ex *turpi causa non oritur actio (no action can be founded on an illegal act).* This principle is based on public policy and may also apply where the claimant's conduct is immoral. The difficulty is deciding which types of conduct are considered sufficiently heinous for the purposes of defence. Some cases have found that it will apply where it would be impossible to determine an appropriate standard of care, whilst others have suggested that the claimant ought not to succeed if to permit him to do so would be an affront to the public conscience.

In *Clunis v Camden and Islington Health Authority* (CA 1998) the plaintiff, who had a long history of mental illness, was convicted of manslaughter and ordered to be detained in a secure hospital. He sued the defendant for negligence for failing to take reasonable care to provide him with after care services following his discharge from hospital where he had been detained under the Mental Health Act 1983.

It was held that, despite a successful plea of diminished responsibility at the criminal trial, his action was barred on the grounds of public policy since he was directly implicated in the illegality and must be taken to have known that what he was doing was wrong.

In *Vellino v Chief Constable of Greater Manchester Police* (CA 2001) the claimant suffered brain damage when he attempted to escape from police custody by jumping though a window on the second floor. Negligence was claimed on the part of the arresting officers, alleging that they had stood by and let him jump. The Court of Appeal held that the claim was untenable because the defendant had to rely on his own criminal conduct in escaping lawful custody to found his claim.

****

Ch. 4

Employer's Liability

This chapter deals with employer's liability for common law negligence to its employees. It should be noted that there are a new set of requirements for employers in relation to health and safety following the Coronavirus Act 2020 and employees return to work.

In addition to common law duty, there is a large body of statutory obligations which the employer has to abide by when protecting its workforce. In relation to accidents and other forms of negligence it is common for employers to sue both in negligence and breach of statutory duty. Employers have a statutory duty to insure against liability, as laid down by the Employers Liability (Compulsory Insurance) Act 1969.

Amendments to the law of strict liability

The then House of Lords introduced legislation to remove the 'strict liability' provisions which mean that companies are automatically liable, regardless of fault, for certain injuries in the workplace. Individuals will now be required to prove negligence on the company's behalf before being able to pursue a claim.

The change was brought into effect on 1 October 2013 and will only apply to injuries incurred after that date. Importantly, pregnant workers are exempted from the amendment and reserve the right to bring a claim for breach of statutory duty in accordance with the Pregnant Workers Directive.

The old regime: strict liability

Under the old regime employees could bring proceedings against their employer for a breach of health and safety regulations unless these regulations said otherwise. This reflected a perception that employees injured at work should be compensated by their employers, who are under a legal obligation to be insured against such possibility, rather than be left with no remedy at all.

Previously, most health and safety regulations imposed strict liability. This means that they could be breached even if the employer has done nothing wrong. For example, Regulation 5 of the Provision and Use of Work Equipment Regulations 1998 requires an employer to ensure 'that work equipment is maintained in an efficient state, in efficient working order and in good repair'. Therefore, an employer would be liable if work equipment failed even if it has been adequately maintained and the failure was not foreseeable.

The new regime: reversing the rules

Section 47 of the Health and Safety at Work Act 1984, by virtue of section 6 of the Enterprise and Regulatory Reform Act 2013, will remove the standard of strict liability from certain health and safety regulations. Going forward, no civil claim may be brought for breach of statutory duty unless a regulation expressly provides for it; this effectively reverses the current position.

In almost all cases it will be for the injured employee to rely on common law negligence and prove that his injuries were caused by the employer's negligence. Negligence is generally a higher hurdle for employees than a breach of statutory duty - particularly those imposing strict liability - as the standard required of employers is higher; greater emphasis is placed on the 'reasonable practicability' defence which balances the expense of potential preventative measures against the scale of the risk.

The removal of strict liability for health and safety breaches is one of many changes designed to combat the perceived 'compensation culture' and reflects a growing trend against punishing employers for injuries that they took all reasonable steps to prevent. Under the present regime businesses have paid out significant sums in compensation with around 78,000 civil liability claims brought each year for injuries sustained at work.

Nature of the duty generally

Although there once existed the doctrine of common employment, in which there was an implied term in a contract of employment that employees accepted risks incidental to their employment, the law has changed significantly.

The doctrine of common employment was abolished in 1948 and, as the law has evolved, employers have a personal duty and a vicarious liability towards their employees. Traditionally, the duty is said to be threefold, which was highlighted in the case of *Wilsons and Clyde Coal Co Ltd v English* (HL 1938), namely "the provision of a competent staff of men, adequate material and a proper system and effective supervision". The duty is not absolute but is discharged by the exercise of reasonable care and is thus similar to the duty of care in the tort of negligence generally. Although most of the cases concern work accidents, the duty extends to guarding against disease and gradual deterioration in health as a result of adverse working conditions. This was illustrated in the case of *Thompson v Smith's Ship repairers (North Shields) Ltd* (HC 1984). However, it does not extend to the prevention of economic loss by, for example, advising the employee to take out insurance nor the prevention of injury to health caused by self-induced intoxication.

Safe plant and equipment

The employer has a duty to take reasonable care to provide proper plant and equipment and to maintain them so as to keep them in good order. This includes the provision of protective devices and clothing appropriate to the job, and also a warning or exhortation from the employer to make use of such equipment.

One case which highlights this is *Bux v Slough Metals Ltd* (CA 1973) where the plaintiff, a foundry worker, lost the sight of one eye when splashed with molten metal. Although the employer had, in compliance with statutory regulations, provided protective goggles, he was held liable for breach of his common law duty, which extended to persuading and even insisting on the use of protective equipment. Most employees will now be protected by the Personal Protective Equipment at Work Regulations 1992, which impose a statutory duty to take all reasonable steps to see that protective equipment is properly used, though it is the employee's duty to use it.

In relation to injury caused by defective equipment, in the case *Davie v New Merton Board Mills Ltd* (HL 1959) it was held that the duty to provide proper tools was satisfied by purchase from a reputable supplier. This decision has now been reversed however, by the Employer's Liability (Defective Equipment) Act 1969, which renders an employer personally liable in negligence if two conditions are met: first, that the employee is injured in the course of his employment by a defect in equipment issued by the employer for the purposes of the employer's business and, secondly, that the defect is attributable wholly or partly to the fault of a third party, (whether identifiable or not. Such a third party could be the manufacturer. Strict liability is thus imposed upon the employer if his employee can prove that some third party was at fault, though contributory negligence can be used as a defence by that third party.

The employee might also be able to rely on the Provision and Use of Work Equipment Regulations 1998 which provide that employers must ensure that work equipment is so constructed or adapted as to be suitable for the purpose for which it is to be used or provided, and that such equipment is maintained in an efficient state.

Safe system of work

A safe system of work means the organisation of work, the manner in which it is to be carried out, the organising and planning of numbers of men and women and their tasks and the instructions given to these workers. One case illustrating this is *Johnstone v Bloomsbury Health Authority* (CA 1991) where it was held that requiring the plaintiff to work such long hours as might foreseeably injure his health could constitute a breach of duty. In *Walker v Nortumberland County Council* (HC 1995) the plaintiff suffered a nervous breakdown as a result of work pressure. Before returning to work it was agreed that assistance would be provided to reduce his workload. Very little was actually provided and he suffered a second breakdown which forced him to stop work permanently. His employers were held liable for failing to provide a safe place of work in that they continued to employ him without adequate assistance. In *Waters v Commissioner of Police of the Metropolis* (2000) the House of Lords held that an employer is under a duty to take reasonable care to protect its employees from harm, including workplace bullying and psychiatric harm, where the employer knows or can foresee that an employee might suffer this harm through the acts of fellow employees.

In *Hatton v Sutherland* (2002) the Court of Appeal ruled that claims for stress induced psychiatric illness follow the standard principles governing personal injury claims in that no special control mechanisms are applied to claims for psychiatric or physical injury arising from stress at work. The ordinary principles of employer's liability apply and the questions to be determined are:

- was there a breach of employer's duty of care which caused psychiatric harm to the employee?
- Was the psychiatric harm to that particular employee reasonably foreseeable?

The duty of care does not arise where the employer is unaware of the employee's vulnerability to stress induced illness or of an imminent psychiatric breakdown.

Safe premises

The employer's obligation includes making the premises as safe as possible. However, the employer is not required to eliminate every foreseeable risk if the burden in so doing is too onerous. In *Wilson v Tyneside Window Cleaning* (CA 1958) where it was held that the duty exists equally in relation to premises in the occupation or control of the third party. In appropriate circumstances an employer must be expected to go and inspect the premises to see that they are reasonably safe for the work to be carried out on them. However, the fact that the employer does not have control of the workplace is important in determining whether he has been negligent. Most workplaces are now governed by the Workplace (Health, Safety and Welfare) Regulations 1992.

Scope of the duty

The scope of the duty relates to the employer-employee and does not extend to an independent contractor. The duty is personal and non-delegable, so that the employer does not discharge his duty by entrusting its performance to another, whether that be an employer or independent contractor.

****

Ch. 5

Vicarious Liability

The general rule here is that a person(s) who expressly authorises or ratifies a tort is expressly liable. However, notwithstanding this, there are other circumstances where a person would be liable for the torts of another person(s) in the absence of this authorisation. This liability is known as vicarious liability.

The employer-employee relationship is the most common example of vicarious liability. The negligence committed by an employee can thus ultimately be the liability of the employer.

Who is an employee?
An employer is only liable for torts committed by his employees and not those committed by an independent contractor so the distinction between the two is important.

The central feature that distinguishes an employee and an independent contractor is not the type of work that they do but the way in which the work is done. The courts have formulated a number of different tests to get to the heart of this distinction.

The control test

The control test distinguishes an employee and an independent contractor on the basis of whether the employer had the right to control the nature of the work done, and, most importantly, how it must be done. *Yewen v Noakes* 1880.

The organisation and integration test

The organisation makes a distinction between a contract of service whereby ' a man is employed as part of the business and his work is done as an integral part of the business' and a contract for services whereby ' work, although done for the business, is not integrated into it but is only accessory to it'.

The courts have also developed what is known as an 'economic reality test', sometimes called the 'multiple test' or the 'pragmatic test'. One case illustrating this is that of *Ready Mixed Concrete Ltd v Minister of Pensions* 1968, where the drivers were hired by the Claimant organisation to deliver concrete using vehicles owned by the drivers which they purchased from the claimant and which had to be painted in company colours and carry the company logo. Drivers were responsible for the maintenance of the vehicles and had flexible hours of work. It was held that the drivers were not employees thus the claimant was not liable for their national insurance contributions.

In this case, it was held that three conditions had to be met before a worker would be considered an employee:

- The employee must provide work or skill for the employer in return for the payment of a wage or some other remuneration.
- The employee agrees, expressly or impliedly, that they will work under the control of the employer

- All other circumstances are consistent with the situation being characterised as a contract of employment.

An employee is employed under a contract of employment. For the employer to be liable, the wrong must be committed in the course of the employee's employment and the employer has authorised the action which results in the tort. The courts will adopt a wide ranging approach to the meaning 'course of employment'. In the case *Century Insurance Co Ltd v Northern Ireland Road Transport Board* (HL 1952) a tanker driver, whilst delivering petrol, lit a cigarette and threw away the match causing a fire. It was held in this case to be the employers liability as this happened in the course of employment.

In the case of Mohamud v WM Morrison Supermarkets Plc (2016) an employee of Morrison supermarkets, Mr Khan, who worked in the kiosk at the supermarket's petrol station, committed a brutal and unprovoked attack on a customer, Mr Mohamud. Mr Khan had responded to an inquiry by Mr Mohamud as to whether it was possible to print some documents by ordering Mr Mohamud to leave the shop, and using threatening and racist language. He had then followed Mr Mohamud to his car, told him never to come back and punched and kicked him. The Supreme Court held the supermarket vicariously liable for the employee's unprovoked violent assault on a customer.

f, however, an employee's act is totally unconnected to the job for which he is employed, the employer is not liable. In the case *Beard v London General Omnibus Co* (CA 1900) the employer of a bus conductor who, in the absence of a driver, negligently drove the bus himself, was held not to be liable. This case contrasts with that of *Kay v ITW Ltd* (CA 1968) where an employee attempted to move a lorry belonging to another firm and which was blocking the entrance to his employer's warehouse to which he had been instructed to return a fork lift. Damage was caused and the employer was held to be vicariously liable as this was done in the course of employment.

Each case will rest on its own merit, with the key factor being whether or not the employee was acting for his/her employer.

Another case, *Lister v Hesley Hall Ltd* (HL 2001) looked more closely at the notion of 'course of employment'. The House of Lords said that the proper approach to the nature of employment is not to ask the simplistic question of whether the acts were modes of doing authorised acts but to adopt a broad assessment and consider whether the torts were so closely connected with the employment that it would be fair and just to hold the employers liable.

In the case *Mattis v Pollock (Flamingos Nightclub)* (CA 2003) the owner of a nightclub was held vicariously liable to the claimant who suffered paraplegia following a stabbing by a doorman employed by the club. The doorman, who had started a fight in the club, went home to get a knife, came back and stabbed the claimant. The stabbing was found to be directly linked to the incident that had happened before and fell within the scope of his employment.

There are cases where the employee's act, although not part of his regular employment as such, is necessarily incidental to it. In the case *Staton v National Coal Board* (HC

1957) an employee cycling to the pay office on the employer's land to collect his pay after work had finished was held to be within the course of his employment

Joint liability

Where an employee commits a tort in the course of his employment, both he and his employer are liable as joint tortfeasers. This essentially means that if the employer satisfies the judgement he may be able to claim a contribution from his employee under the Civil Liability (Contribution) Act 1978.

Independent contractors

In general, an employer is not liable for the negligence of an independent contractor in carrying out his work. He will be liable if he authorises or ratifies the tort.

Vehicle owners

A vehicle owner who allows another to drive his vehicle in his presence makes this person his agent and will be liable for negligent driving. This will be the case even if the person is not present in the vehicle. The case *Launchbury v Morgans* (HL 1973) established that the owner is not liable simply for permitting another to use the vehicle for his own purposes. It must be shown that the driver was using it for the owner's purposes under delegation of some task or duty.

****

Ch. 6

Occupiers Liability

Occupiers have an obligation to ensure that their land is not hazardous to others.

The occupier of a property in respect of loss or injury suffered by those who enter a property or its grounds lawfully is governed by the Occupiers Liability Act 1957 and the Occupiers Liability Act 1984. Prior to these Acts, the extent of liability owed by an occupier depended upon the relationship with the person injured. The OLA 1957 abolished this in favour of two categories:

- Lawful visitors, who were protected by the Act
- All others who were not protected

This Act was supplemented by the Occupiers Liability Act 1984 which covers injuries to trespassers.

Section 2(1) of the 1957 Act provides:

"An occupier owes the same duty, the 'common duty of care' to all his visitors, except in so far as he is free to, and does extend, restrict, modify or exclude his duty to any visitor or visitors by agreement or otherwise".

Who is an occupier?

The Act contains no clear definition of an "occupier". This is simply a term to denote a person who has a sufficient degree of control over premises to put him under a duty of care towards those who lawfully come on to the premises. Control is the decisive factor and it is not material that the occupier has no interest in the land, he could be tenant, lessee, licensee or any other person having the right to possession. One case illustrating this is *AMF International Ltd v Magnet Bowling Ltd* (HC 1968) where building contractors were held to be joint occupiers along with the building owners. A landlord who has let his property to a tenant will not be the occupier of the demised parts but will still be held to be the occupier of those parts, i.e. common parts, not demised to the tenant.

Another key case is *Wheat v Lacon* (1966) House of Lords

The claimant and her family stayed at a public house, The Golfer's Arms in Great Yarmouth, for a holiday. Unfortunately her husband died when he fell down the stairs and hit his head. The stairs were steep and narrow. The handrail stopped two steps from the bottom of the stairs and there was no bulb in the light. The claimant brought an action under the Occupiers Liability Act 1957 against the Brewery company, Lacon, which owned the freehold of The Golfer's Arms and against the Managers of the Pub, Mr & Mrs Richardson, who occupied the pub as a licensee.

Held:

Both the Richardsons and Lacon were occupiers for the purposes of the Occupiers Liability Act 1957 and therefore both owed the common duty of care. It is possible to have more than one occupier. The question of whether a particular person is an occupier under the Act is whether they have occupational control. Lacon had only granted a license to the Richardsons and had retained the right to repair which gave them a sufficient degree of control. There is no requirement of physical occupation. However, it was found that Lacon was not in breach of duty since the provision of light bulbs would have been part of the day to day management duties of the Richardsons. Since the Richardsons were not party to the appeal the claimant's action failed.

In another case *Harris v Birkenhead* (1976) Court of Appeal, the claimant Julie Harris was 4 years old when she wandered off from a children's play park with her friend. They entered a derelict house which was due for demolition. The house had not been secured and the door was open. They went upstairs and Julie sustained serious injury when she fell from a window. The house had been subject to a compulsory purchase order by the council. The house had been owned by a private landlord and the tenant was offered alternative accommodation by the council. The tenant informed the council that she did not want to take up the offer of accommodation and made her own arrangements and left the property. The council served 14 days notice on the owner of their intention to take possession of the property, but never actually took physical possession at the expiry of the 14 days.
Held:
The Council had the legal right to take possession to secure the property, actual physical occupation was not required to incur liability as an occupier. The council were therefore liable.

The premises

The definition of premises is wide and covers not only land and buildings. By s.1 (3)(a) of the Act, the statutory provisions extend to any fixed or moveable structure, including any vessel, vehicle or aircraft. This is apt to include not only structures of a permanent nature but also temporary structures such as ladders and scaffolding.

Visitors

The statutory duty is owed only to visitors who, by s.1 (2) are those who would, at common law, have been either invitees or licensees. For a licence to have been inferred there must be evidence that the occupier has permitted entry as opposed to merely tolerating it, as there is no positive obligation to keep the trespasser out. Repeated trespass of itself confers no licence. However, in some cases the courts have gone to great lengths to infer the existence of a licence. One case illustrating this is *Lowery v Walker* (HL 1911) where members of the public had for many years used the defendant's field as a short cut to the railway station. The defendant had often prevented them from so doing but did nothing further to stop them until, without warning, he turned a savage horse loose in the field. The animal attacked and injured the plaintiff who then sued and succeeded in his action on the basis that he was a licensee not a trespasser.

There are a number of other types of entrant that must be considered. Those who enter premises for any purpose in the exercise of a right conferred by law are treated, by s.2(6) of the Act as having the occupiers permission to be there for that purpose (whether they have it or not). Secondly, s.5(1) provides that where a person enters under the terms of a contract with the occupier there is, in the absence of express provision in the contract, an implied term that the entrant is owed the common duty of care and, according to *Sole v W.J Hallt Ltd* (HC 1973) he may frame his claim either in contract or under the 1957 Act. It is further provided by s.3(1) that where a person contracts with the occupier on the basis that a third party is to have access to the premises, the duty owed by the occupier to such third party as his visitor cannot be reduced by the terms of the contract to a level lower than the common duty of care. Conversely, if the contract imposes upon the occupier any obligation which exceeds the requirements of the statutory duty, then the third party is entitled to the benefit of that additional obligation.

Thirdly, those who use public or private rights of way are not visitors for the purposes of the 1957 Act, though the user of a private right of way is now owed a duty under the Occupiers Liability Act 1984 (see later).

Two interesting cases relating to Non-lawful visitors are *McGeown v Northern Ireland Housing Executive* (1994) House of Lords. The claimant was injured when she tripped in a hole on land owned by the defendant. The land was a public right of way. It was held that the defendant was not liable as the claimant was not a lawful visitor under the Occupiers Liability Act 1957 because she was exercising a public right of way.

Holden v White (1982) Court of Appeal

The claimant, a milkman, was injured on the defendant's land by a manhole cover which broke when he stepped on it. At the time he was delivering milk to the house of a third party who had a right of way across the defendant's land. It was held that he was not entitled to claim against the defendant since he was exercising a right of way and was not therefore a lawful visitor of the defendant.

Exclusions

As has been outlined, the duty owed to a contractual entrant is governed by the terms of the contract and a person who enters under a contract to which he is not party is, at the very least, owed a duty of care. In the case of non-contractual entrants, it is clear that, at common law, an occupier may be able to exclude or limit his liability by notice, provided that reasonable steps are taken to bring it to the visitor's attention and that the notice is clear and not misleading in any way. One case that illustrates this is *Ashdown v Samuel Williams and Sons* (CA 1956) where it was held that the plaintiff, who was injured by the negligent shunting of a railway wagon upon the defendants premises, was defeated in her claim by exclusion notices erected by the defendant saying that person entered at their own risk and no liability would be accepted for loss or damage, whether caused by negligence or otherwise.

The basic principle is that if an occupier can prevent people from entering his premises, then he can equally impose conditions, subject to which entry is permitted. However, the power of the occupier to exclude or restrict his liability for death or injury has been severely reduced by s.2 of the Unfair Contract Terms Act 1977. This section provides that a person cannot, by reference to a contract term or to a notice, exclude or restrict his liability for death or personal injury caused by negligence unless the term or contents of the notice satisfies the requirement of reasonableness.

The operations of s.2 of the Act is confined to those situations where there is business liability which is defined in s.1(3) as liability for breach of duty arising from things done in the course of a business or from the occupation of premises used for the business purposes of the occupier.

Common duty of care

The common duty of care is defined in s.2 (2) as:

"a duty to take such care as in all circumstances is reasonable to see that the visitor will be reasonably safe in using the premises for the purposes for which he is invited or permitted to be there"

This is similar to the common duty of care and may extend to taking steps to see that a visitor does not deliberately harm other visitors by foreseeably likely conduct. Whether the occupier has charged it depends on the facts, taking into account such matters as the nature of the danger, the purpose of the visit and the knowledge of the parties. In particular, there is provision in the act for Children, those with special skills, warning notices and independent contractors.

Children

The Act provides that the amount of care which an occupier can expect from a visitor will depend on certain factors. By s.2(3)(a) the occupier must be prepared for children to be less careful than an adult. However, case law has sought to balance responsibility between occupiers and parents. The level of care expected will depend on the nature of the risk and the age and awareness of the child. For example, in the case *Titchener v British Railways Board* (1983) House of Lords, the Claimant, a 15 year old girl, was out walking with her boyfriend who was 16. They took a short cut across a railway line and they were both hit by a train. He was killed and she was seriously injured. There was a gap in the fence at the place where they crossed and there was a pathway leading to this gap which suggested that there was repeated trespass. Also it was accepted that either the Defendant was aware of the gap or would have been aware upon reasonable inspection. The Defendant raised the defence of *volenti* under s.2(3) of the Occupiers Liability (Scotland) Act 1960

Held:

The scope of the duty owed to trespassers varies on the circumstances. On the facts of this case the Defendants did not owe a duty to a 15 year old trespasser who was fully aware of the risks. Even if the Defendant did owe a duty of care the defence of *volenti* under s.2(3) would succeed.

In Jolley v Sutton (2000) two 14 year old boys found an abandoned boat on land owned by the council and decided to do it up. The boat was in a thoroughly rotten condition and represented a danger. The council had stuck a notice on the boat warning not to touch the boat and that if the owner did not claim the boat within 7 days it would be taken away. The council never took it away. The boys had been working on the boat for 6-7 weeks when one of them suffered severe spinal injuries, resulting in paraplegia, when the boat fell on top of him. The boys had jacked the boat up to work on the underside and the jack went through the rotten wood. The claimant brought an action under the Occupiers Liability Act 1984. The trial judge found for the claimant. The Court of

85

Appeal reversed the decision, holding that whilst it was foreseeable that younger children may play on the boat and suffer an injury by falling through the rotten wood, it was not foreseeable that older boys would try to do the boat up. The claimant appealed.

House of Lords held:

The claimant's appeal was allowed. The risk was that children would "meddle with the boat at the risk of some physical injury" The actual injury fell within that description.

Special skills

Section 2(3)(b) provides that:

"an occupier may expect that a person, in the exercise of his calling, will appreciate and guard against any special risks ordinarily incident to it, so far as the occupier leaves him free to do so".

In the case *Roles v Nathan* (CA 1963) the defendant was held not liable for the death of two chimney sweeps killed by carbon monoxide fumes while sealing up a flue in the defendant's boiler. If the same people had fallen through the floor because of a rotten floorboard the position would have been different.

Warnings

The occupier may, in accordance with s.2(4)(a) of the Act, discharge his duty by warning his visitor of the particular danger, provided that the notice is effective and the warning is sufficient to ensure that the visitor is reasonably safe. Warning notices have to be distinguished from exclusion notices. By sufficient warning the occupier discharges his duty, whereas exclusion purports to take away the right of recovery in respect of a breach.

To be effective a warning must sufficiently identify the source of the danger. A case that highlights this is *White v Blackmore* (1972) Court of Appeal. Mr White was killed at a Jalopy car race due negligence in the way the safety ropes were set up. A car crashed into the ropes about 1/3 of a mile from the place where Mr White was standing. Consequently he was catapulted 20 foot in the air and died from the injuries received. Mr White was a driver in the race but at the time of the incident he was between races and standing close to his family. He had signed a competitors list which contained an exclusion clause. There was also a warning sign at the entrance to the grounds which stated that Jalopy racing is dangerous and the organisers accept no liability for any injury including death howsoever caused. The programme also contained a similar clause. His widow brought an action against the organiser of the event who defended on the grounds of *volenti* and that they had effectively excluded liability.

Held: The defence of *volenti* was unsuccessful. Whilst it he may have been *volens* in relation to the risks inherent in Jalopy racing, he had not accepted the risk of the negligent construction of the ropes. However the defendant had successfully excluded liability (Lord Denning MR dissenting)

There is no duty to warn against obvious risks

Darby v National Trust (2001) Court of Appeal. The claimant's husband, Mr Darby, drowned in a pond owned by the National Trust (NT). The pond was one of five ponds in

Hardwick Hall near Chesterfield. Two of the ponds were used for fishing and NT had taken steps to prevent the use of those ponds for swimming or paddling. However, with regards to the pond in which the fatality occurred, NT had done nothing to prevent visitors using the pond and it was common for visitors to use the pond for paddling and swimming during the warm summer months. On the day in question Mr Darby had been paddling with his children around the edge of the pond. He then swam to the middle to play a game he had often played whereby he would go under water and then bob up to the surface. However, he got into difficulty and drowned. The claimant argued that because of NT's inactivity in preventing swimmers using the pond, both she and her husband had assumed the pond was safe for swimming.

Held:

NT was not liable. The risk to swimmers in the pond were perfectly obvious. There was no duty to warn of an obvious risk.

In *Cotton v Derbyshire Dales District Council* (1994) The claimant, a 26 year old man, had gone out for the day with a group of friends and his fiancé over the Easter bank holiday. They had visited 3 pubs where the claimant had drunk about 4 pints. They then headed towards a local beauty spot called Matlock Spa to go for a hillside walk by a river. The party were in high spirits and became separated. The claimant and his fiancé drifted from the pathway and he was seriously injured when he fell off a cliff. There was a sign at one entrance to Matlock stating "For your own enjoyment and safety please keep to the footpath. The cliffs can be very dangerous, and children must be kept under close supervision." However, there was no such sign at the entrance used by the claimant. The claimant brought an action based on the Occupiers Liability Act 1957 for the failure to adequately warn him of the risk.

Held:

There was no obligation to warn of an obvious risk. The claimant would have been aware of the existence of the cliff so such a warning would not have affected events.

Independent contractors

Where a visitor suffers damage due to faulty construction, maintenance or repair work by an independent contractor employed by the occupier, s 2 (4)(b) provides that the occupier will not be liable if it was reasonable to entrust the work to a contractor and he took such steps as he reasonably ought to see that the contractor was competent and had done the work properly. The occupier is not necessarily expected to check work of a technical nature although in the case of a complex project he may be under a duty to have the contractor's work supervised by a qualified specialist such as an architect or surveyor.

In the case of Ferguson v Welsh (1987) House of Lords Sedgefield District Council, in pursuance of a development plan to build sheltered accommodation, engaged the services of Mr Spence to demolish a building. It was a term of the contract that the work was not to be sub-contracted out. In breach of this term, Mr Spence engaged the services of the Welsh brothers to carry out the demolition who in turn engaged the services of Mr Ferguson to assist. Mr Ferguson suffered serious injury resulting in permanent paralysis when a wall he was standing on collapsed due to the unsafe practices operated by the Welsh brothers. He brought an action against the Council, Mr Spence and the Welsh brothers. The trial judge held that the Welsh Brothers were liable but that Mr Spence and the Council were not liable. Mr Ferguson appealed against the finding against the Council since the Welsh Brothers (or Mr Spence) had the funds or insurance to meet liability.

Held: The appeal was dismissed.

Mr Ferguson was a lawful visitor despite the clause forbidding sub-contracting since Mr Spence would have apparent or ostensible authority to invite him on to the land. However, the danger arose from the unsafe system of work adopted by the Welsh Brothers not the state of the premises. Whilst there was evidence that Mr Spence had sub-contracted demolition work to those executing unsafe practices on previous occasions, there was no evidence that the Council were aware of this.

Defences

The provisions of the Law Reform (Contributory Negligence) Act 1945 apply and s.2(5) of the 1957 Act provides that an occupier is not liable in respect of risks which the visitor willingly accepts, thus allowing for the defence of *volenti non fit inujuria*. However, where there is business liability within the meaning of the Unfair Contract Terms Act 1977, s.2(3) of that Act provides that a person's agreement to or awareness of a notice purporting to exclude liability for negligence is not of itself to be taken as indicating his voluntary acceptance of the risk.

In the case of *White v Blackmore* (1972) Court of Appeal, Mr White was killed at a Jalopy car race due negligence in the way the safety ropes were set up. A car crashed into the ropes about 1/3 of a mile from the place where Mr White was standing. Consequently he was catapulted 20 foot in the air and died from the injuries received. Mr White was a driver in the race but at the time of the incident he was between races and standing close to his family. He had signed a competitors list which contained an exclusion clause. There was also a warning sign at the entrance to the grounds which stated that Jalopy racing is dangerous and the organisers accept no liability for any injury including death howsoever caused. The programme also contained a similar clause. His widow brought an action against the organiser of the event who defended on the grounds of *volenti* and that they had effectively excluded liability.

Held:

The defence of *volenti* was unsuccessful. Whilst it he may have been *volens* in relation to the risks inherent in Jalopy racing, he had not accepted the risk of the negligent construction of the ropes. However the defendant had successfully excluded liability (Lord Denning MR dissenting)

The Occupiers Liability Act 1984

The 1984 OLA extended the protection of the law to cover:

- Trespassers
- People lawfully exercising rights of way
- Visitors to land covered by section 60 of the National Parks and Access to the Countryside Act 1949 and 'right to room' legislation.

The 1984 Occupiers Liability Act governs the liability of an occupier to "persons other than his visitors" in respect of injury suffered by them on the premises due to the state of the premises or to things done or needing to be done to them. The term "persons other than his visitors" includes trespassers and persons exercising private rights of way, but those using public rights of way.

The scope of the duty

Section 1(3) of the 1984 Act provides that the occupier owes a duty if:

a) he is aware of the danger or has reasonable grounds to believe that it exists;

b) he knows or has reasonable grounds to believe that the non visitor is in the vicinity of the danger concerned or that he may come into the vicinity of the danger; and

c) the risk is one against which, in all the circumstances of the case, he may be reasonably expected to offer the non-visitor some protection.

Whilst paragraph (c) clearly adopts an objective test, paragraphs (a) and (b) import a subjective element in that the existence of a duty depends upon the occupiers actual knowledge of facts which should lead him to conclude that a danger exists. If the occupier is not aware of these facts he may not owe a duty.

In the case *Rhind v Astbury* (2004) the claimant accepted that he was a trespasser when he dived into shallow water to retrieve a football, but he argued that his injury was caused by a fibreglass container on the bed of the lake which constituted a danger within the meaning of s.1 (3) of the 1984 Act. The Court of Appeal held that the claimant had failed to establish a duty of care under s.1(3) since the defendant was unaware of the existence of the container and had no reasonable grounds for suspecting that the danger existed.

Another case relating to duty of care is *Donoghue v Folkestone Properties (*2003) Court of Appeal. Mr Donoghue, the claimant, spent boxing day evening in a public house called Scruffy Murphy's. It was his intention, with some of his friends, to go for a midnight swim in the sea. Unfortunately in his haste to get into the water he dived from a slipway in Folkestone harbour owned by the defendant and struck his head on an underwater obstruction, breaking his neck. At his trial evidence was adduced to the affect that the slipway had often been used by others during the summer months to dive from. Security guards employed by the defendant had stopped people from diving although there were no warning signs put out. The obstruction that had injured the claimant was a permanent feature of a grid-pile which was submerged under the water. In high tide this would not have posed a risk but when the tide went out it was a danger. The claimant's action was based on the Occupiers Liability Act 1984. Mr Donoghue was 31, physically fit, a professional scuba diver who had trained in the Royal Navy. It was part of his basic knowledge as a diver that he should check water levels and obstructions before diving. The trial judge found for the claimant but reduced the damages by 75% to reflect the extent to which he had failed to take care of his own safety under the Law Reform (Contributory Negligence) Act 1945. The defendant appealed contending that in assessing whether a duty of care arises under s.1(3) each of the criteria must be assessed by reference to the individual characteristics and attributes of the particular claimant and on the particular occasion when the incident in fact occurred ie when assessing whether the defendant should be aware of whether a person may come into the vicinity of the danger, it should be assessed on the likelihood of someone diving into the water in the middle of the night in mid-winter rather than looking at the incidences of diving during the summer months.

Held:

Appeal allowed. The test of whether a duty of care exists under s.1(3) Occupiers Liability Act 1984 must be determined having regard to the circumstances prevailing at the time of the alleged breach resulted in injury to the claimant. At the time Mr Donoghue sustained his injury, Folkestone Properties had no reason to believe that he or anyone else would be swimming from the slipway. Consequently, the criteria set out in s.1(3)(b) was not satisfied and no duty of care arose.

It is to be noted that the statutory duty applies only to personal injury or death. Liability for loss of, or damage to, property is expressly excluded by s. 1(8).

Defences

Section 1(5) of the Act provides that the occupier may, in appropriate cases, discharge his duty by taking reasonable steps to warn of the danger or to discourage persons from incurring the risk. Whether a warning is effective will depend among other things upon the nature of the risk and the age of the entrant.

The defence of *volenti non fit injuria* is preserved by s.1(6) of the Act. It is normally limited to dangers arising from the state of the premises. The plaintiff was held to have willingly accepted the risk as his own, within the meaning of s.1(6) of the Act in the case of *Rathcliffe v McDonnell* (CA 1999). (page 96) In this case, the plaintiff, having drunk four pints agreed to go open-air swimming with his friends. He climbed over the gate of a college swimming pool. Although conscious of a warning sign he dived in the pool and suffered horrific injuries as a result.

The Court of Appeal rejected his claim for damages on the grounds that he was aware of the risk and had willingly accepted it.

Standard of care

S.1(4) OLA 1984 - the duty is to take such care as is reasonable in all the circumstances of the case to see that the other does not suffer injury on the premises by reason of the danger concerned.

In Revill v Newbery (1996) Court of Appeal, Mr Newbery was a 76 year old man. He owned an allotment which had a shed in which he kept various valuable items. The shed was subject to frequent break ins and vandalism. Mr Newbery had taken to sleeping in his shed armed with a 12 bore shot gun.

Mr Revill was a 21 year old man who on the night in question, accompanied by a Mr Grainger, went to the shed at 2.00 am in order to break in. Mr Newbery awoke, picked up the shot gun and fired it through a small hole in the door to the shed. The shot hit Mr Revill in the arm. It passed right through the arm and entered his chest. Both parties were prosecuted for the criminal offences committed. Mr Revill pleaded guilty and was sentenced. Mr Newbery was acquitted of wounding. Mr Revill brought a civil action against Mr Newbery for the injuries he suffered. Mr Newbery raised the defence of *ex turpi causa*, accident, self-defence and contributory negligence.

Held:

The Claimants action was successful but his damages were reduced by 2/3 under the Law Reform (Contributory Negligence) Act 1945 to reflect his responsibility for his own injuries.

Ratcliff v McConnell and Harper Adams College (1997) Court of Appeal

The claimant was a student at Harper Adams College. One night he had been out drinking with friends on campus and they decided they would go for a swim in the college pool which was 100 yards from the student bar. They climbed over a locked gate into the open air swimming pool. The pool had a notice at the entrance which stated the pool would be locked and its use prohibited between the hours of 10pm -6.30am. There was a notice at the shallow end in red on a White background stating 'Shallow end' and a notice at the deep end stating 'Deep end, shallow dive'. However, the boys did not see the signs because there was no light. The three boys undressed. The claimant put his toe in the water to test the temperature and then the three of them lined up along the side of the pool and dived in. Unfortunately the point at which the claimant dived was shallower than where the other boys dived and he sustained a broken neck and was permanently paralysed. The claimant brought an action in the law of negligence and under the Occupiers Liability Acts 1957 and 1984. The trial judge held that the claimant was a trespasser since he was not permitted to go into the pool and that the College owed a duty of care under the 1984 Act since the pool had often been used by students in the prohibited hours so the College should have been aware that the claimant was within a class of persons who may come into the danger. The breach was in not taking more preventative action to prevent use of the pool. The claimant's damages were, however, reduced by 60% under the Law Reform (Contributory Negligence) Act 1945. The defendants appealed contending the evidence relied on by the claimant in terms of repeated trespass all took place before 1990 before they started locking the gates.

Held:

The appeal was allowed. The claimant was not entitled to compensation.

The defendant had taken greater steps to reduce trespass by students since 1990. The only incidence of trespass to the pool in the four years prior to the claimant's injury, related to students from a visiting college and therefore there was no reason for the college to suspect the students had come into the danger so no duty of care arose under s.1(3)(b) Occupiers Liability Act 1984. Also the trial judge had incorrectly identified the danger. The pool itself was not dangerous it was the activity of diving into it which was unsafe. This was an obvious danger to which there was no duty to warn. By surrounding the pool with a 7 foot high fence, a locked gate and a prohibition on use of the pool in the stated hours the College had offered a reasonable level of protection.

The duty may be discharged by giving a warning or discouraging others from taking the risk S.1(5) Occupiers Liability Act 1984 - note there is no obligation in relation to the warning to enable the visitor to be reasonably safe - contrast the provision under the 1957 Act.

Exclusion notices

There is no mention in the Act of excluding liability to the non-visitor, and the provisions of the Unfair Contract Terms Act 1977 do not apply to the 1984 duty. Trespassers pose problems because depending upon the point at which they enter the premises, they may be less likely to see a notice than a lawful visitor. One suggested solution is that the duty under the 1984 Act is a minimum which cannot be excluded so that even the lawful visitor would be protected by it, even though he was aware of an exclusion notice.

Independent contractors and trespassers

At common law, the liability of a contractor to the trespasser rests upon ordinary negligence principles. The fact that the claimant is a trespasser in relation to the occupier is not relevant except in so far as the trespassers presence may be less foreseeable. One case which illustrates this is *Buckland v Guildford Gas Light and Coke Co* (HC 1949). The defendants, who had erected electricity cables on a farmer's land close to the top of a tree, were held liable for the death of a young girl who climbed the tree and was electrocuted.

Breach of statutory duty

Breach by the defendant of an obligation under statute (other than one which expressly seeks to impose liability in tort) may, apart from giving rise to any criminal sanction laid down in the Act, also enable a person injured by the breach to bring a civil action for damages for breach of statutory duty. This is a tort in its own right independent of any other form of tortuous liability. Whether a claimant can sue depends on whether the statute confers a right of civil action, or can be interpreted as conferring this right.

The claimant must prove that the legislature intended to create a right to sue. In *Cullen v Chief Constable of the Royal Ulster Constabulary* (2003) the House of Lords upheld the previous decisions that the claimant could not rely on the tort of breach of statutory duty for the failure of the police to give him reasons for delaying his access to a solicitor, on the ground that the duty concerned could be enforced through judicial review. In a few instances, Parliament has expressly made known its intention, but in the majority of cases statute is silent on the issue. It is for the courts to decide what the intention of an Act is and, to this end, certain guidelines have been established. The basic proposition is that a breach of statutory duty does not, by itself, give rise to a private law action. Such an action will arise, however, if it can be shown that, on the proper construction of the statute, the duty was imposed for the protection of a limited class of the public and Parliament intended to confer upon members of that class a right to sue for breach. There is no general rule for determining whether the Act does create such a right, but if no other remedy is provided for its breach that is an indicator in the claimant's favour. If the Act does contain other provision for enforcing the duty that is an indication of an intention that it was to be enforced by those means alone and not by private law action. In determining whether, in any particular case, a civil action for breach of statutory duty will lie, the starting point is to look at precedent or for a clearly stated Parliamentary intention. In the absence of either it is in all cases a question of ascertaining the fundamental purpose the legislation intended to achieve, and that can only be done through a consideration of the Act as a whole.

****

Ch. 7

Liability for Dangerous/Defective Products

Defective products can give rise to liability in a variety of ways. Claims may arise in contract law or consumer law involving various statutes, most commonly the Consumer Rights Act 2015, which came into force on October 1st 2015. It is worth noting that there is a distinction between causes of action in contract and tort in relation to defective products. In relation to tort, liability can arise either under the common law in negligence or under the Consumer Protection Act 1897.

Part 1 of the Consumer Protection Act 1987, which came into force on 1st March 1988, creates a strict liability for dangerous goods.

Part 1 was enacted to give effect to an E.C. Directive of 1985, requiring the harmonisation of law on product liability throughout the E.C. If the Act doesn't apply in certain circumstances a claimant may still be able to sue for negligence.

When claiming damages for harm suffered as a result of a defective product, the claimant must prove that he or she suffered damage caused wholly or partly by a defect arising from a specific product.

The Act (s.2.(2)) outlines who the potential defendants might be in such cases:

a) the producer of the product;

b) any person who holds himself out to be a producer by putting his name or trade mark or any other distinguishing mark on the product;

c) an importer of the product into a Member State from a place outside the E.C. in order to supply it to another in the course of his business.

The term 'producer' is defined in s.1(2) to mean either the manufacturer, or the person who won or extracted the product, or, where the product has not been manufactured, won or abstracted but the essential characteristics of which are attributable to an industrial or other process having been carried out, the person who carried out that process.

Furthermore, by s.2(3) the mere supplier (e.g. Retailer) is liable if he fails within a reasonable time to comply with the plaintiff's request to identify one or more of the persons to whom s.2(2) applies, or to identify his own supplier.

'Product' is defined in s.1(2) as any goods or electricity. Component parts and raw materials also fall within the definition of product as distinct from the overall product in which they are comprised. For example, the brakes in a car would be the responsibility of both manufacturer of brakes and the supplier of the finished car.

The meaning of 'defect'

A product is defective, according to s.3(1) if its safety is not such as persons are generally entitled to expect. The safety of a product expressly includes safety "with respect to products comprised within that product" (i.e. components and raw materials) and a product may be unsafe not only if there is a risk of personal injury but also if it poses a risk of damage to property. When determining what people are entitled to expect, s.3(2) provides that account shall be taken of all the circumstances including the following specific matters:

a) the way in which and the purposes for which the product has been marketed, its get-up, and warnings and instructions for use accompanying it:
b) what might reasonably be expected to be done with or in relation to the product;
c) the time when the product was supplied by its producer to another.

The reference in (a) to the purposes for which the product has been marketed may indicate that a balance has to be struck between known risks associated with a product and the benefits which it seeks to confer. With regard to (b), a product which is clearly intended for a particular use may not be defective if it causes damage when put to an entirely different use. With (c) it is the time of supply by the producer to another which is relevant not the time of supply to the consumer.

Liability under the Act is considerably stricter that under common law. One case that illustrates this is *A and others v National Blood Authority* (2001). The claimants had been infected with Hepatitis C, through blood transfusions which had used blood products obtained from infected donors. The defendants argued that the product was as safe as might be expected, and also that the defect in the particular transfusion could not have been detected). Given the strict liability under the Act, it was held that factors which would have been relevant in a negligence action were completely irrelevant and the defendants were found to be liable under the Consumer Protection Act.

Definition of "damage"

Section 5(1) defines damage for the purposes of Part 1 as death or personal injury, or loss of or damage to property (including land), although claims for damage to property are limited in several respects. First, the defendant will not be liable for damage to the defective product itself, nor for damage to any product supplied with a defective component comprised in it. Secondly, there is no liability unless, at the time of the damage, the property was "of a description of property ordinarily intended for private use, occupation of consumption" and was intended by the claimant mainly for such purposes (s.5(3)). A person who suffers damage to his business property must therefore sue in negligence as opposed to under the Act.

Finally, no claim will succeed where its value is less than £275, excluding interest.

Defences

Section 4(1) of the Act provides for defences as follows:

a) The defect is attributable to compliance either with a domestic enactment or community law.
b) The defendant did not at any time supply the product to another. A broad definition is given to "supply" in a later part of the act to include not only the usual types of supply contract but also gifts.

c) The defendant supplied the product otherwise than in the course of his business and either he does not fall within s.2(2) (he is not a producer, "own brander" or importer) or he does so only by virtue of things done other wise than in a view to profit.

d) The defect did not exist at the relevant time. By s.4(2) the "relevant time" means, in relation to electricity, the time at which it was generated. With all other products it means, in the case of a defendant to whom s.2(2) applies the time when he supplied the product to another and, in the case of a supplier, the time of the last supply by a person who is within the ambit of that section.

e) The state of scientific and technical knowledge at the relevant time was not such that a producer of products of the same description as the product in question might be expected to have discovered the defect if it had existed in his products while they were under his control. This is called the "development risk" or "state of the art" defence

f) The defect constituted a defect in a product containing the defendant's component part (or raw material) and was wholly attributable to the design of the overall product or to compliance by the defendant with instructions given by the producer of the overall product.

Common law negligence

Where the Consumer Protection Act does not apply, the claimant must rely on existing common law remedies. If the claimant acquires defective goods under a sale or similar supply contract the remedy is to sue the supplier for breach of implied undertakings relating to quality. Although these contractual obligations are generally imposed only upon those who supply in the course of business, they are strict and entitle the claimant to recover both in respect of goods which simply fail to work or which are less valuable than those contracted for, and where the defect causes personal injury or damage to property. If the claimant does not have a contract, an action in tort may be pursued.

The duty of the manufacturer

The duty owed by a manufacturer to the consumer was stated in Donoghue v Stevenson (Hl 1932) by Lord Atkins as follows:

"A manufacturer of products, which he sells in such a form as to show that he intends them to reach the ultimate consumer in the form in which they left him with no reasonable possibility of immediate examination, and with the knowledge that the absence of reasonable care in the preparation or putting up of the products will result in an injury to the consumer's life or property, owes a duty to the consumer to take that reasonable care".

The term "products" includes not only comestibles, but many other diverse products such as shoes, vehicles, toys and so on. the manufacturer's duty extend to the packaging of the product and to any labels, warnings or instructions for use which accompany it. If the manufacturer of a finished product incorporates a component made by another, he is under a duty to check on its suitability and may be liable for failure to do so should it turn out to be defective. Where products are already in circulation when the defect is discovered the manufacturer must take reasonable steps to warn of the danger or to recall the products.

Manufacturer and ultimate consumer

The term "manufacturer" has been interpreted to include any person who actively does something to the goods to create the danger, such as assemblers, servicers, repairers, installers and erectors.

In *Malfroot v Noxal Limited* (HC 1935) an assembler was held liable when the side car which he had negligently fitted to a motor cycle came adrift and injured the plaintiff. Mere suppliers may come within the rule, even though they may be unaware of the danger and do nothing to create it. In the case *Andrews v Hopkinson* (HC 1957) a second hand car dealer was liable for failing to check that an 18 year-old car was roadworthy, with the result that the plaintiff was injured in a collision caused by a failure of the steering.

Apart from the end user of the product, the "ultimate consumer" is any person who may foreseeably be affected by it. In the case *Stennet v Hancock and Peters* (HC 1939) the defendant was held liable for negligently fitting a metal flange to a wheel of a lorry, so that it came off when the vehicle was in motion and struck the plaintiff.

Proof of negligence and damage

The burden rests upon the claimant as in any other negligence action. However, damage caused by a defect in manufacture as opposed to a defect in design, may easily give rise to an inference of negligence. On the other hand, if it is equally probable that the defect arose after the manufacturing process and is wholly unconnected with anything that the manufacturer may have done, claimant will fail.

The defendant will no longer escape liability however, merely by showing that he had a fool-proof system of manufacture and quality control, because the very fact of the defect may be evidence of negligence in the operation of that system by a person for whom the defendant is vicariously liable. Where the alleged defect is in relation to the design of the product, the claimant may face greater difficulty in that the issue of negligence is to be judged in the light of current knowledge which must be proved to have been such as to render the damage foreseeable.

As far as damage is concerned, liability only exists in respect of personal injury or damage to other property, although consequential financial loss is also recoverable. Pure economic loss is, however, irrecoverable.

****

Ch. 8

Nuisance

For the purposes of an action in tort a nuisance may be either private (affecting a particular individual or property) or public (impacting on a wider group of people). In addition, there is a large number of statutory provisions aimed at the control of conduct which is damaging to the environment some of which impose civil liability in respect of certain hazards.

Private nuisance

The claimant may bring an action in private nuisance where the defendant unlawfully interferes with his use or enjoyment of his land or of some right that he may have in relation to it. The usual complaint is that of "invasion of land" as a result of something that the defendant has done on his own land. The distinction between this sort of invasion and trespass is that in this case the invasion is indirect. Causing physical damage to the land or buildings/vegetation on it constitutes a nuisance. In this case, the interference is evidenced by tangible physical damage.

It is equally a nuisance to interfere with a neighbours right to quiet enjoyment of his land. This may take a variety of forms, such as smell, dust, smoke, noise and vibration. In the case *Thompson-Scwab v Costaki* (CA 1956) the use of a house in a respectable residential area was found to be actionable.

The law seeks to achieve a balance between two competing interests, that of the defendant to use his land as he wishes and that of his neighbour not to be seriously inconvenienced. Not every inconvenience is actionable because a degree of tolerance is expected in the interests of peaceful co-existence. Interference becomes unlawful only where the defendant has put his land to unreasonable use. Where, however, the alleged nuisance causes tangible damage the claimant will usually have little difficulty in establishing unlawful interference with his rights

Unreasonable interference

Lord Denning, in *Miller v Jackson* (CA 1977) stated "the very essence of a private nuisance...is the unreasonable use by a man of his land to the detriment of his neighbour". The defendant's actual or constructive knowledge of that detriment is a factor in determining whether the interference is unreasonable but a number of other factors, including the character and duration of the interference, must also be considered. Whether the defendant has unreasonably used his land cannot be gauged solely by reference to the nature of his conduct, because some foreseeable harm may be done which the law does not regard as excessive between neighbours under a principle of "give and take, or live and let live".

In regarding the issue of reasonable use, the court may have regard to the following:

1. Degree of interference

Where physical damage to property has been done, a relatively small interference may amount to a nuisance, but in other cases, the interference must be substantial. One case that illustrates this is *Walter v Selfe* (HC 1851) in which the test was said to be whether there was "an inconvenience materially interfering with the ordinary comfort physically of human existence, not merely according to elegant or dainty modes and habits of living, but according to plain and sober and simple notions among the English people" It is therefore a question of degree as to whether the interference is sufficiently serious. One case illustrating this is *Halsey v Esso Petroleum Ltd* (HC 1961) where the defendants were held liable for nuisance caused by a nauseating smell emanating from their factory and by the noise at night from the plant and from arriving and departing tankers.

2. Nature of the locality

The nature of the locality will have a significant bearing as a person living in an industrial town or city cannot expect the same freedom from noise or pollution, but this is not a relevant consideration where there is physical injury to property. In *St Helens Smelting co v Tipping* (HL 1865) the defendant's were held liable for the emission of fumes from their factory in a manufacturing area which proved injurious to the plaintiff's shrubs. Conversely, in *Murdoch v Glacier Metal Co Ltd* (CA 1998) night time factory noise was held not to constitute an actionable nuisance having regard to all the circumstances including the proximity of the plaintiff to a busy by-pass.

3. Social utility

The mere fact that the defendant's act is of benefit to the community will not in itself relieve the defendant of liability.

It is a question of degree and if the damage is substantial or there is physical damage the public interest should not be allowed to prevail over private rights. For example, in the case *Adams v Ursell* (HC 1913) the smell from a fried fish shop was held to constitute a nuisance to nearby residents, notwithstanding the defendants argument that he was providing a valuable service to poor people in the neighbourhood.

4. Abnormal sensitivity

A man cannot increase the liabilities of his neighbour by applying his own property to special uses, whether for business or pleasure (*Eastern and South African Telegraph Limited v Cape Town Tramways Co Limited* (PC 1902). In the case *Robinson v Kilvert* (CA 1889) warm air from the defendant's premises increased the temperature in an upper part of the building and caused damage to stocks of brown paper which the plaintiff stored there. The amount of heat was not such to cause annoyance to those working for the plaintiff, nor was it harmful to paper generally so the plaintiff's action failed. The same principle applies to sensitive persons, and no regard is had to the particular needs of individuals such as those with an acute sense of smell or hearing.

5. State of affairs

The interference must be continuous or recurrent rather than temporary or occasional. Duration of interference and times at which it occurs are important factors in deciding whether a nuisance exists.

An isolated escape is probably not actionable as a nuisance though it may show evidence of the existence of a dangerous state of affairs upon the defendant's land. One case illustrating this is *Spicer v Smee* (HC 1946) where defective electrical wiring which started a fire and caused damage to adjacent property was held to constitute a nuisance. *In Crown River Cruises Ltd v Kimbolton Fireworks Ltd* (HC 1996) the holding of a firework display in circumstances where it was inevitable that for 15-20 minutes burning debris would fall on an adjacent property of a potentially flammable nature was held to constitute a nuisance.

6. Intentional annoyance
If the defendant has as his aim the express purpose of annoying his neighbour, he will be liable, even though the degree of interference would not constitute a nuisance in the ordinary course of events.

7. Damage
Damage must usually be proved, either in the form of tangible injury to land or property upon it, or in the form of amenity damage as evidenced by substantial personal discomfort.

Who is liable?

Person creating the nuisance
The creator of the nuisance is liable whether or not he occupies the land from where the nuisance emanates. He remains liable even if he parts with possession and is no longer able to stop the nuisance without trespass.

The occupier

The occupier will be liable if he creates the nuisance, but, apart from this, he may incur liability in respect of the acts of others upon his land or where the nuisance existed before he became the occupier

Although it is a general rule that an employer will not be liable for the defaults of his contractor, he will be liable if he is under a non-delegable duty, as where there is a withdrawal of support from neighbouring land or operations are conducted on or adjoining the highway, *Tarry v Ashton* (HC 1876).

Trespassers

If a nuisance is created by a trespasser, the occupier is liable not only if he adopts the nuisances for his own purposes but also if, with actual or constructive knowledge of its existence, he fails to take reasonable steps to abate it. This principle was laid down in *Sedleigh-Denfield v O'Callaghan Ltd* (HL 1940) and has since been extended to dangerous states of affairs which arise naturally upon the land. In the case *Goldman v Hargrave* (PC 1967) a tree on the defendant's land was struck by lightening and caught fire. The defendant had the tree felled and decided to let the fire burn itself out, but it eventually spread to the plaintiff's land causing damage. The defendant was liable because with actual knowledge of the danger, he failed to take reasonable steps to abate it.

The landlord

Where premises are let the usual person to sue is the tenant. However, the landlord will be liable if he expressly or impliedly authorises the nuisance.

In the case *Smith v Scott* (HC 1973) a local authority was held not to have authorised the commission of a nuisance by a 'problem family' which it had housed next to the plaintiff. Further, in the case *Hussain v Lancaster City Council* (CA 1999) the council was not liable in respect of a long term campaign of racial harassment on a shopkeeper by the local authority's tenants because the act complained of did not involve the use of the tenants land.

The landlord is liable if either he knew or ought to have known of the nuisance before letting the premises. If the premises fall into disrepair during the period of the tenancy the landlord is liable if he has reserved the right to enter and carry out necessary repairs.

Apart from common law obligations the landlord may be liable under the Defective Premises Act 1972, s.4. This provides that if the landlord is under an obligation to his tenant to repair. Or has an express or implied power to enter and repair, he owes a duty to take reasonable care to see that all who might reasonably be expected to be affected by defects in the state of the premises are reasonably safe from personal injury or damage to their property.

The Human Rights Act 1998

A common law nuisance can constitute an interference with the claimant's rights under Art 8 of the European Convention on Human Rights (respect for private and family life) and/or Protocol 1, Article 1 (protection of property). Obviously, when considering the principles of human rights a balance has to be struck between different and competing interests.

One case that illustrates this is *Marcic v Thames Water Authorities* (HL 2003). Sewers provided by Thames Water had caused flooding which discharged both surface water and foul water on the claimant's garden. Many thousands of other householders were at risk of flooding as a consequence of the discharge from overburdened sewers in the Thames area. Thames Water claimed that the cost of the work required to alleviate the flooding would result in expenditure in excess of £100 million and they sought to rely on lack of resources to justify their decision to take no steps to abate the nuisance. In the first instance the judge dismissed the claims against Thames Water. He also concluded that the failure by Thames water to carry out suitable repair work gave no cause for action for breach of statutory duty. However, he held that the failure of Thames Water to repair the sewer constituted an interference with the claimant's rights under the Human Rights Act.

The Court of Appeal held that this was not a human rights claim at all, although the claimant was entitled to succeed under the common law of nuisance and agreed with the judge that the defendant had acted incompatibly with the claimant's Convention rights.

The case reached the House of Lords (now Supreme Court) and they held that the claimant did not have a common law action in nuisance and further held that his claim under the Human Rights Act to be null and void as there was no infringement on his rights under the European Convention on Human Rights.

Essentially, the Human Rights Act does not afford absolute protection as it is far too broad and can be too literally interpreted. Each case on its own merit.

Public nuisance

A public nuisance may be defined as an unlawful act or omission which materially affects the comfort and convenience of a class of citizens who come within the sphere of its operation. At common law, public nuisances cover a wide variety of activities such as carrying on an offensive trade, selling food unfit for human consumption and obstructing the highway.

There are two requirements that must be satisfied:

- the nuisance has affected a class of people
- the claimant has suffered special damage

Public and private nuisance

Public nuisance is a crime in respect of which the Attorney General may, if a criminal prosecution is felt to be inadequate, bring a 'relator' action for an injunction to retrain the offending activity.

The same conduct may amount to both a public or private nuisance, but an individual may only sue in tort in respect of the latter if he has suffered 'particular' damage which means loss or damage over and above that suffered by the rest of the class of citizens affected. This encompasses personal injury and there is no requirement that the claimant has an interest in land.

Nuisance on the highway

The most common form of nuisance is obstruction or interference with the public's right of passage along the highway. In the case, *Castle v St Augustine's Links* (HC 1922), for example, the defendant's golf club was held liable for siting one of its fairways so that golf balls were frequently sliced on to the highway, with the result that the plaintiff was injured when driving along the road when a golf ball crashed through the windscreen of his car. In another case, *The London Borough of Wandsworth v Railtrack PLC* (CA 2001) droppings from feral pigeons roosting under a railway bridge created a hazard over the footpath and to pedestrians and therefore constituted a public nuisance.

In relation to obstructions, the defendant is liable only if he creates an unreasonable risk, but he is generally liable for the defaults of his contractor.

A highway authority is under a duty to maintain the highway and may be liable in negligence, nuisance or breach of statutory duty under the Highways Act 1980. This right of action for non-repair does not, however, extend to claims for pure economic loss. The Act provides that it shall be a defence to prove that the authority had taken such care as in all the circumstances was reasonably required to make sure that the art of the highway to which the action relates was not dangerous for traffic. Neither does the authority owe a duty of care to exercise its statutory powers for the benefit of road users.

Remedies for nuisance

The principal remedies for nuisance are damages and injunctions. Damages are available to compensate a claimant for physical damage to his land and in relation to personal discomfort and inconvenience.

The claimant may recover damages for any resulting loss which is of a reasonably foreseeable kind. An injunction can be granted against the perpetrator if damages in themselves cannot immediately remedy the problem.

****

Ch. 9

Defamation

Defamation Defined

Defamation is a tort which protects a person from loss of reputation by prohibiting the publication of information likely to attract negative attention from others.

Further, defamation is defined as the publication of a statement which tends to lower a person's standing and also damages self-esteem. It will also encourage others to avoid that person.

In the case Berkoff v Burchill (CA 1996), for example, the Court of Appeal (majority) held that to describe an actor and director of films as "hideously ugly" was capable of being defamatory in that it could lower his standing in the public's estimation and make him an object of ridicule.

Although a trading organisation can sue for defamation, local government, political parties and other organs of government cannot, because to allow them to do so would inhibit freedom of speech. The ultimate aim of the law is to arrive at a balance between freedom of speech and defamation of character.

Further, although actions are usually tried before a jury (although see below, section 11 of the Defamation Act 2013), the court may, in accordance with the Defamation Act 1996, dispose summarily of the claim if either it has no realistic chance of success or there is no viable defence. In the case of no viable defence the court may give judgement for the plaintiff, which by s.9 may include damages of up to £10,000.

Although defamation and the misuse of private and personal information are both torts which can be relied on by any individual it tends to be more well known people whose cases have a higher profile, usually in conflict with the media. This highlights the difficulty of the law to balance between two clearly conflicting rights: the right of the individual to privacy (Article 8 of the European Convention on Human Rights) and the media's right to freedom of expression (Article 10).

The Defamation Act 2013
Why was the Act introduced?
The Defamation Act 2013 was introduced in order to reform the law surrounding defamation and to ensure that a fair balance between the protection of reputations and freedom of expression was being attained. Whilst the previous law sought to protect reputations by preventing derogatory statements from being made about individuals, it hindered free speech and protected powerful people from scrutiny. It was argued that the law of defamation was being used as a means to silence individuals and that too much restriction was being placed upon the ability to express oneself.

Many attempts were made by the courts to strike a balance between the right of the individual to privacy and the media's right to freedom of expression.

The most prominent case in this respect was that of **Reynolds v Times Newspapers Ltd (2001.)** The so-called *Reynolds test* emanates from the judgment of the House of Lords in

Reynolds v Times Newspapers. Albert Reynolds was a former Irish Prime Minister accused in the British press of deliberately misleading the Irish Parliament. Reynolds sued for defamation and the defendants pleaded, inter alia, qualified privilege (see below).

At the trial the jury returned a verdict in the plaintiff's favour and he was awarded the sum of 1p by way of damages. The Court of Appeal set aside the jury's verdict and ordered a retrial. The court also ruled that the publication was not covered by qualified privilege. The defendants appealed, arguing that there should be a 'generic' qualified privilege encompassing the publication by a newspaper of political information. The House of Lords rejected this argument. They considered that the proposed new category of qualified privilege would fail to provide adequate protection for reputation. In addition they held that it would be unsound in principle to distinguish political discussion from other matters of serious public concern. However, they did say that the defence of qualified privilege would be available in respect of political information when the defendant satisfied the old common law test, i.e.:

"where the person who makes a communication has an interest or a duty, legal, social, or moral, to make it to the person to whom it is made, and the person to whom it is so made has a corresponding interest or duty to receive it."

Lord Nicholls, giving the leading judgment, went on to provide a non-exhaustive list of the factors to take into account when deciding whether the defence should be available:

"1. The seriousness of the allegation. The more serious the charge, the more the public is misinformed and the individual harmed, if the allegation is not true.

2. The nature of the information, and the extent to which the subject-matter is a matter of public concern.

3. The source of the information. Some informants have no direct knowledge of the events. Some have their own axes to grind, or are being paid for their stories.

4. The steps taken to verify the information.

5. The status of the information. The allegation may have already been the subject of an investigation which commands respect.

6. The urgency of the matter. News is often a perishable commodity.

7. Whether comment was sought from the plaintiff. He may have information others do not possess or have not disclosed. An approach to the plaintiff will not always be necessary.

8. Whether the article contained the gist of the plaintiff's side of the story.

9. The tone of the article. A newspaper can raise queries or call for an investigation. It need not adopt allegations as statements of fact.

10. The circumstances of the publication, including the timing."

The application of these factors came to be known as the Reynolds test. This test also led in time to the introduction of the Draft Defamation Bill in March 2011 which contained provisions to 'reform the law to strike the right balance between protection of freedom of speech and protection of reputation' which subsequently resulted in the enactment of the 2013 Defamation Act.

Changes to the Law

Section 1 of the Defamation Act 2013 introduces a 'serious harm' test for all defamation claims. Under this new test, a statement will not be considered defamatory unless it can be shown that its publication would cause, or be likely to cause, serious harm to the reputation of the individual. Whilst this provision seeks to ensure that only the most serious of statements are considered defamatory, it will need to be considered what is meant by 'serious harm' which could create some ambiguity. Still, this section of the Act is likely to 'deter applicants from raising frivolous defamation actions.'

Section 2 of the Act repeals section 5 of the Defamation Act 1952 by abolishing the common law defence of justification and introducing a defence of 'substantial truth.' If a defendant can demonstrate that the statement which they have made is 'substantially true' then they will be capable of relying on this defence. This section seeks to ensure that protection is also being provided to the freedom of speech by allowing statements of truth to be made. *Section 3* of the Act repeals section 6 of the Defamation Act 1952 by abolishing the common law defence of fair comment and providing a defence of 'honest opinion.' Thus, if the defendant can show that the statement made was an honestly held opinion then this section can be relied upon.

Section 4 abolishes the common law defence created in the **Reynolds** case which seemed to provide a new immunity for the media and introduces a statutory public interest defence. This section allows for statements to be made that are said to be a matter of public interest provided that the maker of the statement believed this to be the case. It has been argued that this section reduces flexibility and will be likely to create additional litigation, though it seems as though the section just puts the **Reynolds** defence on a statutory footing.

Section 5 of the Act creates a new defence to an action for defamation brought against the operator of a website hosting user-generated content where the action is brought in respect of a statement posted on the website. The Section 5 defence applies if the operator can show that the operator did not post the statement on the website. However, the defence is defeated if the person bringing the claim (the claimant) can show: - that it was not possible for the claimant to identify the person who posted the statement (that is, the claimant did not have sufficient information to bring legal proceedings against the person); - that the claimant gave the operator a notice of complaint in relation to the statement; and - that the operator failed to respond to that notice in accordance with the procedure set out in the Defamation (Operators of Websites) Regulations 2013.

The Section 5 defence will also be defeated if the claimant can show that the operator acted with malice in relation to the posting of the statement, but is not defeated just because the operator moderates statements posted on the website.

Section 6 Provides protection for academics and scientists publishing in peer reviewed journals, the content of which is privileged under certain conditions.

Section 7 Updates and extends the circumstances in which the defences of absolute and qualified privilege are available.

Section 8 – Single publication rule. Claimants are prevented from bringing an action in relation to publication of the same material by the same publisher after the expiry of a one year limitation period from the date of the first publication of that material to the public, or a section of the public.

Section 9 'Libel tourism'. This provides that a court does not have jurisdiction to hear and determine an action in defamation unless it is satisfied that, of all the places in which the statement complained of has been published, England and Wales is clearly the most appropriate place in which to bring an action in respect of the statement.

Section 10-Secondary publishers. This section prohibits actions for defamation brought against secondary publishers (such as booksellers) except when it is not reasonably practible for the claimant to bring the action against the author, editor or publisher.

Section 11-Jury trials. This section removes the presumption of trial by jury.

The Act appears to have codified existing common law rules and principles, thereby making it easier to determine when a defamation action is capable of taking effect. This is supposed to provide the courts with the ability to strike a balance between defamation and freedom of speech so that both interests can receive adequate protection.

Libel and slander

A defamatory statement or representation in permanent form is a libel. However, if conveyed by spoken words or gestures, this is a slander. Apart from the written word, pictures, statues and other effigies can be libels. In addition, radio and television broadcasts are treated as publication in permanent form (The Broadcasting Act 1990) as are words spoken during a public theatrical performance (Theatres Act 1968).

Reading out a defamatory statement to a third party is seen to be a libel. Defamatory statements on record or tape are seen as slander. As we have seen above, section 1(1) of the Defamation Act 2013 added a 'serious harm' element to the common law test: a defamatory statement is now only available if it causes serious harm (or is likely to cause serious harm) to the claimant's reputation.

An important distinction between libel and slander is that libel is actionable per se without proof of special damage, whereas slander requires proof of such, except in the following cases. First, a direct imputation of a criminal offence punishable in the first instance with prison. Second, an imputation that the plaintiff is presently suffering from a contagious or infectious disease, likely to cause others to shun him. Thirdly, an imputation of unchastity to any women or girl (Slander of Women Act 1891). Fourthly, words calculated to disparage the claimant in any office, trade, calling or business held or carried on by him at the time of the publication. The common law requirement that the words had to be spoken in the way of the claimant's calling has been removed by s.2 of the Defamation Act 1952.

Apart from these exceptions, slander requires proof of special damage. The damage must not be too remote.

What must be proved

Whether the action is for libel or slander the claimant must prove that a defamatory statement referring to him was published. The words must be defamatory in accordance with the definition already given, though it need not be proved that anyone who actually heard or read them believed them to be true. Where the statement tends to discredit the claimant only with a special class of persons, he may not succeed unless people generally take the same view. For example, in

Byrne v Deane (CA 1937) it was held not to be defamatory to say of a club member that he had informed the police of an illicit gambling machine on the club premises, because right thinking persons would not think less well of such a man. The circumstances in which the statement is made might be important. Words spoken at the height of a violent quarrel are, for example, not actionable if those who hear them saw them as mere abuse at the time. The question is one of interpretation.

In the case of *Charleston v News Group Newspapers Ltd (HL 1995)* the defendants published a potentially defamatory headline and photograph, but the text of the accompanying article plainly negated the defamatory meaning. The plaintiff was held to have no cause of action because of the fact that the article was well balanced.

Reference to the claimant

There must be a sufficient indication that the claimant is the subject of the statement and in most cases, at least where the claimant is named, this presents no real difficulty. The claimant need not be named however, nor need there be any pointer in the statement indicating that it is the claimant being referred to, provided that people may reasonably draw the inference. In respect of a statement aimed towards a class of persons (i.e. surveyors) no individual member of that class may usually sue unless there is some indication in the words, or the circumstances of their publication, which indicates a particular person. If the reference is to a small class, such as company directors of a specific company they all may sue.

Publication

There must be publication to at least one other person than the claimant or the defendant's spouse. There is no publication by a typist or printer merely by handing the article back to its author. Every repetition of a defamatory statement is a fresh publication so that, as regards printed matter, the author, editor and publisher are all liable. At common law, a mechanical distributor of print, such as a library or newsagent is presumptively liable but will have a defence if he can prove that he did not know that the work contained libel and that lack of knowledge was not due to negligence in the conduct of his business.

Publication includes websites *(Johnson v Steele (2014)* tweets and re-tweets *(Mcalpine v Bercow 2012)* and blogs *(Cruddas v Adams 2013).*

Innocent publication

It is not defamation for a person, who is not the author, editor or publisher of the material, to reproduce material that they did not believe contained defamatory comment provided that they took reasonable care in publishing the statement: section 1 of the Defamation Act 1996.

In *Bunt v Tilley (2007)* it was held that an internet service provider which performed no more than a passive role in facilitating postings on the internet could not be deemed to be a publisher at common law. However, in *Tamiz v Google Inc (2013)* the Court of Appeal held that Google was the 'second publisher' of a third party blog once the defamatory nature of comments on the London muslim blog had been brought to its attention.. As we have seen, section 5 of the Defamation Act

2013 also introduced 'notice and takedown' procedures for website operators.

In another case, *Godfrey v Demon Internet (1999)* the defendant Internet Service provider did not dispute the defamatory nature of the statement but claimed that it was not responsible for postings by the users on its Internet sites. Although the defendant was held not to be the publisher within the meaning of s.1 of the Defamation Act 1996, there was liability in this case because the claimants had notified the defendant of the defamatory content of the message and requested that it be removed. The defendants failed to remove the message and were unable to rely on the defence in s.1 of the Act which required them to show that they had exercised reasonable care in relation to the publication.

Defences

Justification or truth is usually an absolute defence, although the analogous common law defence of 'justification' was replaced by section 2 of the Defamation Act 2013, which provides that it is a defence to an action for defamation for the defendant to show that the imputation conveyed by the statement complained of is substantially true.

The onus is on the defendant to prove the truth of the statement. He need only show that the statement is substantially true. Whether the defence falls through a minor inaccuracy is a matter for the jury. S.5 of the Defamation Act 1952 provides that the defence does not fail if the truth of a number of charges cannot be proved, provided that the words proved not to be true do not materially damage the claimant's reputation having regard to the truth of the remaining charges.

Where the defendant's allegation is that the claimant has been convicted of an offence, section 13 of the Civil Evidence Act 1968 (as amended by s.12 of the Defamation Act 1996) provides that proof that he stands convicted of it is conclusive evidence that he did commit it.

Honest opinion

The common law defence of fair comment applied to critical comment based on the facts. It generally involved media comments about matters of public interest and the defence regarded that the person making the comment must have believed it to be based in truth and must not have been acting maliciously.

In *Lowe v Associated Newspapers Ltd (2007)* the court set out the relationship between fact and comment:

- in order for a defendant to be permitted to rely upon the defence of fair comment, readers of the words complained of must be able to distinguish facts from comment, either because the facts had been set out or referred to in the words complained of, or because the facts were sufficiently widely known for readers to recognise the comment as statement; and

- the ultimate test of a defence of a fair comment was the objective one of whether someone could have expressed the commentators defamatory opinion upon the facts known to the commentator, at least in general terms and upon which he was purporting to comment.

The common law defence of fair comment was replaced by section 3 of the Defamation Act 2013, 'Honest Opinion' which provides that the defence applies when:

- the statement complained of was a statement of opinion
- the statement complained of indicated, whether in general or specific terms, the basis of the opinion
- an honest person could have held the opinion on the basis of true facts or alleged true facts held under opinion.

Unlike the common law defence, there is no requirement for the statement to be made with malice or on a matter of public opinion.

Privilege

Privilege refers to those circumstances in which it is regarded as imperative that people are able to express their views without fear of legal action. As such, it represents the primacy of the interests of freedom of expression over the rights of the individual in protecting his reputation.

Absolute privilege

Statements made on occasion of absolute privilege are not actionable regardless of whether the defendant was malicious. They include the following:

Statements made in the course of parliamentary proceedings including reports and papers ordered to be published by either house. Members of Parliament may now, by virtue of s.13 of the Defamation Act 1996, waive Parliamentary privilege for the purpose of bringing proceedings.

Statements made during the course of judicial proceedings, whether by judge, jury, counsel or witnesses, provided they are broadly relevant to the issue before the court. The privilege extends not only to proceedings in an ordinary court of law, but to any tribunal recognised by law and acting in a similar manner, even though it is not empowered to take a final decision on the issue.

Communications between solicitor and client in connection with litigation.

Communications by one officer of state to another in the course of his official duty.

By s.14 of the Defamation Act 1996 fair and accurate reports of proceedings in public before any court in the United Kingdom, the European Court of Justice, the European Court of Human Rights or any international criminal tribunal set up by the United Nations. The report must be published contemporaneously along with the proceedings.

Statutory protection is given to various reports of the Parliamentary Commissioner for Administration and of Local Commissioners.

Qualified privilege

This defence exists in respect of statements made for the protection of one's private interests or for the protection of the public interest, as where a complaint is laid before the proper authorities to secure the redress of a public grievance.

It is also available were the maker of the statement and the recipient have a common interest in the matter, or where the recipient alone has an interest and the maker is under a legal, moral or social duty to communicate as, for instance, where a reference is given to a prospective employer. The common thread in all of these instances is that the defendant has either an interest in making, or a duty (legal, social or moral) to make the statement But an equally essential requirement is that the person to whom the statement is made must either have a reciprocal interest or be under a corresponding duty to receive it.

A case that illustrates this is *Watt v Longsdon (CA 1930)*.The director of accompany, the defendant, received a letter from A, a manager of the company, which was defamatory of the plaintiff, who was managing director. The defendant replied to A in terms defamatory of the plaintiff and he also published A's letter to the company chairman and to the plaintiff's wife. In a libel action against the defendant it was held that his letter to A was privileged because both had a common interest in the company's affairs. The communication of A's letter to the chairman was also privileged on the grounds that the defendant was under a duty to report the matter. However, the defendant was held to be under no duty to communicate the letter to the plaintiff's wife.

In addition to the above, a number of reports are protected, including fair and accurate reports of parliamentary proceedings and of public judicial proceedings. A number of fair and accurate reports and statements receive qualified privilege by s.15 of the Defamation Act 1996. These reports are found in schedule 1 to the Act and are divided into two categories, the first being privileged without "explanation or contradiction" and the second "subject to explanation or contradiction".

Qualified privilege may be lost if the defendant publishes the statement more widely than is necessary for the protection of an interest. However, a publication by a defendant to a third party who has no interest or duty is nevertheless protected if it is reasonable and in the normal course of business. The defence is also lost upon proof that the defendant was actuated by malice which may either mean lack of honest belief in the truth of the statement or use of the privilege for an improper purpose.

Sections 6 and 7 of the Defamation Act 2013 deal further with the protection under privilege-particularly section 6 which extends protection to material published in peer reviewed journals.

Remedies- Damages

The primary remedy for a successful claimant is damages which, unusually, are determined by the jury following the issue of guidelines by the judge about the likely impact of their decision. The Courts and Legal Services Act 1990 provides that the quantum of damages can be reassessed by the Court of Appeal if the award by the jury is inappropriate, such as the reduction from £250,000 to £110,000 in Rantzen v Mirror Group Newspapers (1994).

Injunction

There are two rules for injunction in defamation cases, as outlined in Bonnard v Perryman (1891):

- An interlocutory injunction can be obtained to prevent publication of defamatory material if the claimant is aware that this is likely.
- An injunction can be sought after a successful defamation claim if the claimant can establish that there is a real risk of repetition of the publication.

In Greene v Associated Newspapers (2005) it was held that the rule from Bonnard v Perryman did not constitute an infringement of Article 8 of the European Convention on Human Rights (Privacy). The Human Rights Act 1998 had not affected the rule that a court would not grant an interlocutory injunction to restrain the publication of an alleged defamatory statement unless it was clear that the alleged libel was untrue.

****

Ch. 10

Strict Liability

Although the law of tort is mainly fault based there are instances in which liability may be imposed without negligence on the defendant's part. For example, there may be strict liability for damage caused by defective products and animals. Also, an employer's vicarious liability for the torts of its employees is not dependant on fault on part of the employer. Strict liability is also imposed by certain statutes. However, as we have seen in chapter 4, there have been amendments to the rule of strict liability for employers, coming into force from 2013.

Examples of strict liability

The causes of action which attract strict liability include:

- breaches of the General Data Protection Regulation, the Data Protection Act 2018, and its predecessor, the Data Protection Act 1998
- infringement of intellectual property rights, including
- the statutory rights granted by copyright, patent, designs (both registered and unregistered) and trade mark infringement
- the common law tort of passing off
- an action in equity to prevent to misuse or unauthorised disclosure of confidential information
- vicarious liability which applies in, for example employment relationships.

- An employer is strictly liable for the acts and omissions of an employee where the employee acts (or fails to act) in the course of their employment
- product liability
- defamation
- procuring a breach of contract
- the tort of conversion, and
- the law of bailment.
- Strict liability also applies in torts where a common design exists between the defendants: that is, civil conspiracy.

Strict Liability in Contracts

Breaches of agreements - contracts - also attract strict liability. However, it's not a tort. But defences may be available under the terms of the contract itself, by reference to the conduct of the party claiming damages, or both. A party to a contract which breaches the agreement is strictly liable for its breach.

Damages for breach of contract are awards for the breach of contract, regardless of fault on the part of the offending party, which are assessed by:

- the loss caused by the breach
- the remoteness of the loss (i.e. the Rule in Hadley v Baxendale)
- whether the claimant has mitigated its loss

The rule in Rylands v Fletcher (HL 1868)

Although the rule had its origins in nuisance it had, until recently, come to be regarded as having evolved into a distinct principle governing liability for the escape of dangerous things. The Rylands principle has more recently been restated with certainty in *Transco v Stockport Metropolitan Borough Council* (2003) Where the House of Lords held that the strict liability rule, which had stood for nearly 150 years, should not be discarded. The rule was stated by Blackburn J as follows:

" We think that the true rule of law is, that the person who for his own purposes brings on his lands and collects and keeps there anything likely to do mischief if it escapes must keep it in at his peril, and if he does not do so, is *prima facie* answerable for all the damage which is the natural consequence of its escape"

The House of Lords added the qualification that the defendant must have put his land to a non-natural use.

There is no liability for an escape of things naturally upon the land such as self-grown vegetation. The defendant may however be liable in nuisance or negligence and will also be liable if instrumental in causing the escape of something natural to the land.

The rule has been applied to a wide variety of things including water, gas, electricity, fire, explosions and so on.

Escape
There must be an "escape from a place where the defendant has occupation or control over land to a place which is outside his occupation or control" *Read v J. Lyons and Co Ltd* (HL 1947). In the case mentioned above, Transco (2003) the House of Lords held that there had been no escape when the water which leaked from the council's service pipe remained on its land. The defendant need not have any interest in the land from which the thing escapes.

Defences

An Act of God is an operation of natural forces "which no human foresight can provide against, and of which human prudence is not bound to recognise the possibility" However, this is not to say that the defendant will escape liability merely because the event is not reasonably foreseeable. Two cases illustrate this: In *Nichols v Marsland* (CA 1876) the defendant was held not liable when an exceptionally violent rainfall caused the artificial ornamental lakes to flood his neighbour's land. This decision was criticised in *Greenock Corp v Caledonian Rye* (HL 1917) where, on similar facts, the defendant was held liable on the ground that it was insufficient for him to show that the occurrence was one which could not reasonably be anticipated. He must go further and prove that no human foresight could have recognised the possibility of such an event.

Act of a stranger

The defendant is not liable if the escape is due to the unforeseen act of a third party over whom they have no control. In the case *Rickards v Lothian* (PC 1913) the occupier of a lavatory was not liable when an unknown person deliberately blocked up the overflow pipe and caused flooding on the plaintiff's premises. The defence is not available if the act is one which the defendant ought reasonably to have foreseen and guarded against. In the case *Northwestern Utilities Ltd v London Guarantee and Accident Co* (PC, 1936) the defendant's gas main was fractured by a local authority in the course of constructing a sewer. The defendant's were held liable in negligence for damage caused by an explosion of gas because they knew of the work being carried out and, in view of the risks involved, should have checked to make sure that no damage had been done to their mains

For the purposes of this defence, a trespasser is a stranger but employee's in the course of their employment and independent contractors are not.

Consent of the claimant

Express or implied consent to the consent of the dangerous thing is a defence unless the defendant was negligent. Consent may be implied where a thing is brought on to the land for the common benefit of the claimant and defendant.

Default of the claimant

If the claimant's own act or default causes the damage no action will lie. In the case *Dunn v Birmingham Canal Navigation Co* (EC 1872) the claimants persisted in working their mine beneath the defendant's canal and failed in their action when water flooded the mine. Where the claimant is partly at fault the defence of contributory negligence will apply. If damage is caused only by reason of the extra-sensitive nature of the claimant's property he may not be able to recover.

The escape of fire

At common law a person was liable if a fire spread from his premises and did damage to adjoining premises, though there is some doubt as to whether or not liability was strict. He is now liable where the fie is caused by negligence or nuisance, or where it starts and spreads as a result of a non-natural user of land, in which case negligence need not be proved.

There is an defence in respect of a fire caused by an act of God or a stranger, though the defendant may be under a duty to abate a known danger upon his land.

Statute

The Fires Prevention (Metropolis) Act 1774 provides that no action shall lie against a person upon whose land a fire accidentally begins. This provision only applies to fires produced by mere chance or incapable of being traced to any cause. No protection is afforded when the fire is caused negligence or is due to a nuisance or arises from a non-natural user of land. Nor will liability be escaped if there is negligence in permitting an accidental fire to spread. In the case *Musgrave v Pandelis* (CA 1999) the defendant was held liable when a fire started in the carburettor of his car in a garage without fault on anyone's part and his chauffeur negligently failed to extinguish it.

****

Ch. 11

Liability for Animals

A person may incur liability for damage caused by animals in accordance with the ordinary principles of tort.

For example, in the case *Draper v Hodden* (CA 1972) the defendant's terriers savaged an infant. The defendant was held liable for failing to confine them. A defendant is generally not liable if animals naturally upon her land escape and do damage to her neighbour unless he was at fault permitting their accumulation.

Strict liability for dangerous animals
The Animals Act 1971 contains specific rules relating to the keeping and control of animals. The 1971 distinguishes between dangerous and non-dangerous animals.

The Dangerous Wild Animals Act 1976
The Dangerous Wild Animals Act 1976 requires keepers of dangerous wild animals to take out compulsory insurance policies against liability for damage caused to third parties and to be licensed by the local authority.

Dangerous species of animals
By s.2(1) of the Act the keeper of an animal belonging to a dangerous species is liable for any damage caused by it. A dangerous species is one which is not commonly

domesticated in the British Isles and whose fully grown animals normally have such characteristics that they are likely, unless restrained, to cause severe damage (6.(2)). Once a species of animal has been classified as dangerous the law takes no account of the fact that an individual animal within that species may in fact be harmless. A trained circus elephant will not be treated any differently to an elephant in the bush.

Strict liability is therefore imposed by s.2(1). There is no indication in the Act as to what the test for remoteness should be. However, it is held that as long as a causal link is established between the animal and the damage, there is no need for the damage to be of a kind normally associated with the animal. For example, in the case *Tutin v Chipperfield Promotions Ltd* (HC 1980) the defendant was held liable for injuries suffered as a result of a fall from a swaying camel.

Animals not belonging to a dangerous species

Strict liability is imposed in s.2(2) of the Act for animals not belonging to a dangerous species. The keeper is liable for damage caused by such an animal if:

a) the damage is of a kind which the animal, unless restrained, was likely to cause or which, if caused by the animal, was likely to be severe; and

b) the likelihood of the damage or of its being severe was due to characteristics of the animal which are not normally found in animals of the same species, or are not normally so found except at particular times or in particular circumstances; and

c) those characteristics were known to the keeper or to any person in charge of the animal at the time as the keeper's servant or, where that keeper is the head of the household

One case which illustrates the above is that of *Curtis v Betts* (CA 1990), where the plaintiff was attacked and bitten by the defendant's dog, a bull mastiff, as it was being put into the defendant's car. With respect to (a) above, it was found that although the damage in question was not of a kind which this dog, unless restrained, was likely to cause, a bite from a bull mastiff was likely to be severe. In relation to (b) it was found that the dog, in common with its breed generally, was territorially defensive, and that the likelihood of damage being severe was thus due to characteristics which would not be found in bull terriers except in particular circumstances (for example, when defending their territory). On evidence, the defendant knew of his dog's characteristics and was held liable under the Act although he was not found to be negligent.

In another case, *Smith v Ainger* (CA 1990) the keeper of a dog with a known propensity to attack other dogs was held liable to a plaintiff who was knocked over and injured by the dog in the course of its attack upon the plaintiff's dog.

For the purposes of (c) the keeper must have actual, not merely constructive, knowledge of his animal's characteristics.

The keeper

Liability under s.2 is imposed upon the keeper who, by s.6(3), is the person who owns the animal or has it in his possession or is the head of the household of which a member under the age of 16 owns it or has it in his possession. If a person ceases to own or have possession of the animal he will remain the keeper until such time as another person becomes the keeper. Therefore, those who abandon unwanted pets do not divest themselves of responsibility. A person who takes possession of an animal to prevent it from causing damage or to return it to its owner, does not, merely by doing so become its keeper.

Defences

Apart from contributory negligence, which is preserved under s.10 of the Act, s.5 of the Act contains a number of defences. There is no liability if the damage is wholly due to the claimant's fault (s.5(1)) or he voluntary assumes the risk thereof (s.5(2)). An important ,imitation on the defence is that, by s.6(5), a keepers employee is not to be treated as voluntarily accepting risks incidental to employment. Section 5(3) applies to trespassers and provides that the keeper is not liable for damage done by an animal to persons trespassing upon the premises if either the animal was not kept there to protect persons or property or, if it was kept for that purpose, it was not unreasonable to do so.

This will not affect the liability which a person may incur as an occupier under the Occupiers Liability Act 1984. Further, the Guard Dogs Act 1975 makes it a criminal offence to keep a guard dog on business premises (but not on agricultural land or land surrounding a private dwelling) unless either it is secured or under the control of a handler.

Dogs attacking livestock

Section 3 of the Animals Act imposes strict liability upon the keeper of a dog which causes damage by killing or injuring livestock. It is a defence under s.5(4) that the livestock was killed or injured on land on to which it had strayed and the dog belonged to the occupier or its presence was authorised by him.

There is a defence is s.9 of the Act to an action for killing or injuring a dog. The defendant must prove that he acted for the protection of livestock and was entitled to do so, and that within 48 hours she notified the police. A person is entitled to act for their protection if either the livestock or the land on which it is belongs to him. He acts for protection only if either of the following conditions apply:

a) the dog is worrying or is about to worry the livestock and there are no other reasonable means of ending or preventing the worrying; or

b) the dog has been worrying livestock, has not left the vicinity, is not under anyone's control, and there are no practical means of ascertaining to whom it belongs.

The defence in s.9 applies only to the protection of livestock from marauding dogs, so that if damage is caused to property by other animals, or if some reason the statutory provisions are not satisfied, the defendant may fall back on the common law. This entitles the defendant to take punitive action if the animal is actually attacking his property or there is imminent danger that it will renew an attack already made, and it is reasonable in the circumstances for the protection of that property to kill it.

Straying livestock

By s.4 (1) of the Act where livestock belonging to any person strays on to land owned or occupied by another and causes damage to the land or property the person to who the livestock belongs is liable for damages. He will also be liable for reasonable expenses incurred by the other person in keeping the livestock while it cannot be restored to the person to which it belongs.

There is no liability under section 4 for personal injuries or third party property damage, which means that if such damage is caused the action must be brought either in negligence or, if appropriate, under s.2(2) of the Act.

Other

By s.4(1) of the Act where livestock belonging to any person strays on to land owned or occupied by another and causes damage to the land or property in the ownership or possession of the other person, the person to whom the livestock belongs is liable for the damage. He will also be liable for reasonable expenses incurred by the other person in keeping the livestock while it cannot be restored to the person to whom it belongs.

An occupier on to whose land livestock has strayed has a right under, and subject to the conditions of s.7 to detain and, ultimately, to sell the livestock to recover the cost of damage done to his property.

Common law immunity in respect of damage caused by animals straying on to the highway from adjacent land is abolished by s.8(1) of the Animals Act with the result that liability is now determined in accordance with ordinary negligence principles. A landowner is not necessarily obliged to fence land. If he does not then there are important factors in deciding whether negligence has occurred, such as prevailing traffic conditions, whether any warning has been given and what users of the highway ought reasonably to expect.

In particular, by s.8(2) if he has a duty to place his animals on unfenced land he will not be in breach of a duty of care merely by placing them there, so long as the land is in an area where fencing is not customary or is common land or is a town or village green.

The Dangerous Dogs Act 1991, as amended

The Dangerous Dogs Act 1991, as amended by the 1997 Dangerous Dogs Amendment Act, became law in the UK as a response to a growing number of incidents involving serious injury and death as a result of an attack by dogs, often involving children. The law is in force in England, Wales and Scotland, with Northern Ireland passing the Dangerous Dogs Order, which is similar. the Act bans certain breeds of dog which are considered dangerous and shouldn't be owned as pets.

Dogs covered by the Act

It is now illegal to own, sell or breed any of the following:

- The Pit Bull Terrier (any dog known as a pitbull type)
- Japanese Tosa
- Dogo Argentino
- Fila Brasiliero

The Act also covers cross breeds and mixed breeds, with ancestry from the above four dogs, and also those having significant physical characteristics or traits of the breeds in question.

****

Index

****